CONFORMED
TO HIS IMAGE
&
THE SERVANT
AS HIS LORD

Discovery House Publishers

Books, music, and videos that feed the soul with the Word of God

Box 3566 Grand Rapids, MI 49501

CONFORMED TO HIS IMAGE
&
THE SERVANT AS HIS LORD

Lessons On Living Like Jesus

Oswald Chambers

Author of *My Utmost for His Highest*

Conformed to His Image
Copyright © 1950 Oswald Chambers Publications Association

The Servant as His Lord
Copyright © 1957 Oswald Chambers Publications Association

This edition copyright © 1996 Oswald Chambers
Publications Association Limited

Discovery House Publishers is affiliated with RBC Ministries,
Grand Rapids, Michigan 49512

Unless indicated otherwise, Scripture quotations are from The New
King James Version. Copyright © 1979, 1980, 1982, Thomas Nelson
Publishers, Inc.

Library of Congress Cataloging-in-Publication Data

Chambers, Oswald, 1874–1917.
    Conformed to his image & the servant as his Lord : lessons on living
like Jesus / Oswald Chambers.
        p. cm.
    Previously published: Fort Washington, Pa. : Christian Literature
Crusade ; Grand Rapids, Mich. : Chosen Books, 1985.
    ISBN 1-57293-020-9
    1. Sermons, English. I. Title.
BV4253.C457   1996
233—dc20   96–34431
                                                                CIP

Printed in the United States of America

05 06 07 08 09 / CHG / 11 10 9 8 7

CONTENTS

PUBLISHER'S FOREWORD

There is no record of anyone ever falling asleep during a talk by Oswald Chambers. Surely it must have happened, but it's hard to imagine nodding off while listening to a man whose winsome life and dynamic words conveyed the reality of Christ to believers or skeptics. Never content to spout theory, Chambers brought every message to an issue of willful allegiance to the One who died on the cross that we might have His life in us, and be "sons and daughters of God, with a strong family likeness to Jesus."

The talks in this combined volume were given to students at the Bible Training College in London (1911–1915), to members of the League of Prayer in various meetings across Britain, and to soldiers at the Zeitoun YMCA Camp (Egypt) during World War I (1915–17). A careful reading will reveal a repetition of basic themes throughout the book. Chambers was primarily a teacher, and he gave his listeners more than one opportunity to grasp his main point. Regardless of audience and location, Chambers maintained his focus on the Person of Christ and the life He places within all who receive Him.

This book is published with the prayer that it will bring every reader fresh hope and encouragement as a follower of Christ.

The Publisher

FOREWORD TO
THE SERVANT AS HIS LORD

This book has a message for our time. There is much discernment of the state of our age at its closing period. "What is described in the climax is true in every stage till the climax is reached." Jesus Christ foretold tribulation to His followers. But God gives us a fighting chance of winning through to triumph, and there is much here to nourish and guide His saints in their hours of conflict. There is much also about a saint's inner life—the soul of a Christian. The soul is the same in every age. It can be self-pervaded, or influenced by Satanic power, or God-possessed. There is also a remarkable exposition of the closing verses of Romans 8. We get a glimpse into the deep things of life. And we learn much about the principalities and powers that encircle us but are not to conquer us. There is a lovely parable of the making of bread used to illustrate the making of saints and a word about the patience of the saints in a whirl of tumult.

The four sections have appeared as separate booklets, but in this form they fuse into one great message making clear the truth that the Lord's servant may be, and should be, "as his Lord."

David Lambert

CONFORMED
TO HIS IMAGE

Christian Thinking

I cannot soar into the heights you show,
Nor dive into the deeps that you reveal;
But it is much that high things are to know,
That deep things are to feel.

Jean Ingelow

The safe position in Christian thinking is to remember that there are deeper depths than we can fathom, higher heights than we can know; it keeps us reverent, keeps us from hardening off into a confined, cabined experience of our own.

Thinking is not of first importance; life is of first importance. Neither in natural nor in spiritual life do we begin by thinking. Christian thinking means thinking on the basis of things, not thinking in pious terms. With many the experience is right, the life of God is there, but there has been no thinking on the basis of things, and when things hit, there is confusion. If we are going to think along Christian lines and know where to place our individual experiences, it is time we exercised ourselves intellectually as well as spiritually.

Redemption

The Gospel to me is simply irresistible. Being the man I am, being full of lust and pride and envy and malice and hatred and false good, and all accumulated exaggerated misery—to me the Gospel of the grace of God, and the Redemption of Christ, and the regeneration and sanctification of the Holy Ghost, that Gospel is to me simply irresistible, and I cannot understand why it is not equally irresistible to every mortal man born of woman.

Pascal

Redemption is the great outside fact of the Christian faith; it has to do not only with a person's experience of salvation, but with the basis of one's thinking. The revelation of redemption means that Jesus Christ came here in order that by means of His death on the cross He might put the whole human race on a redemptive basis, so making it possible for everyone to get back into perfect communion with God. "I have finished the work which You have given Me to do" (John 17:4). What was finished? The redemption of the world was complete. People are not going to be redeemed; they are redeemed. It is finished. It was not the salvation of individual men and women like you and me that was finished: the whole human race was put on the basis of redemption.

Do I believe it? Let me think of the worst individual I know, the one for whom I have no affinity, the one who is a continual thorn in my flesh, who is as mean as can be; can I imagine that person being presented perfect in Christ Jesus? If I can, I have got the beginning of Christian thinking. It ought to be an easy thing for the Christian who thinks to conceive of any and every kind of person being presented perfect in Christ Jesus, but how seldom we do think! If I am an earnest evangelical preacher I may say to someone, "Oh, yes, I believe God can save you," while in my heart of hearts I don't believe there is much hope for him. Our unbelief stands as the supreme barrier to Jesus Christ's work in people's souls. "Now He did not do many mighty works there because of their unbelief" (Matthew 13:58). But once let me get over my own slowness of heart to believe in Jesus Christ's power to save, and I become a real generator of His power to others. "Nor is there salvation in any other, for there is no other name under heaven given among men by which we must be saved" (Acts 4:12)—the solitary, incommunicable place of Jesus in our salvation! Are we banking in unshaken faith on the redemption, or do we allow men's sins and wrongs to so obliterate Jesus Christ's power to save that we hinder His reaching them? "He who believes in Me . . . ," that is, active belief based on the redemption, ". . . out of his heart will flow rivers of living water" (John 7:38). We have to be so faithful to God that through us may come the awakening of those who have not yet realized that they are redeemed.

We must distinguish between the revelation of redemption and the experience of regeneration. We don't experience life; we are alive. We don't experience redemption; we experience regeneration, that is, we experience the life of God coming into our human nature, and as soon as the life of God comes in it produces a surface of consciousness, but redemption means a great deal more than a person is conscious of. The redemption is not only for humankind, it is for the universe, for the material earth; everything that sin and the devil have touched and marred has been completely redeemed by Jesus Christ. There is a day coming when the redemption will be actually manifested, when there will be a new heaven and a new earth, with a new humanity upon it. If redemption is confounded with regeneration, we get confused. In the majority of cases people have had an experience of regeneration, but they have not thought about what produced the experience, and when the great revelation fact of the redemption is expounded there is misunderstanding. All that an individual experiences is believing in Jesus, but that experience is the gateway into the awe and wonder of the knowledge of God. "And this is eternal life, that they should know You the only true God" (John 17:3).

The Bible deals with the fundamental underlying things of human life, and one of these fundamental things is the presence of a disposition of sin in every person. *Solidarity* means oneness of interests, and the phrase, "the solidarity of the human race," indicates that there is an underlying connection running straight through human life; on the religious side this connection is the heredity of sin, which was introduced into the world through one man, not by the devil—"Therefore, just as through one man sin entered the world . . . because all sinned" (Romans 5:12). When the apostle Paul says, "Knowing this, that our old man was crucified with Him" (Romans 6:6), he is referring to this heredity. Through the redemption we have deliverance from the disposition of sin that is within us and severance from the body of sin to which we are connected by the "old man"; that is, we are absolutely and completely delivered from sin both in disposition and in domination: "having been set free from sin" (verse 18) Unless the universality of sin is recognized we will never understand the need for the redemption. What the redemption deals with is the sin of the whole human race, not primarily with the sins of individuals, but something far more fundamental—the heredity of sin. Pseudoevangelism singles out the individual, it prostitutes the terrific meaning of the redemption into an individual possession, the salvation of *my* soul.

The basis of Christian thinking is that God has redeemed the world from the possibility of condemnation on account of the heredity of sin, "God was in Christ reconciling the world to Himself, not imputing their trespasses to them" (2 Corinthians 5:19). The revelation is not that Jesus Christ was punished for our sins, but that "He made Him who knew no sin to be sin for us, that we might become the righteousness of God in Him" (verse 21). God nowhere holds a man responsible for having inherited the disposition of sin any more than he is held responsible for being born. We have nothing to do with our birth or with what we inherit, because we had no choice in either. A person will say, "If I am not held responsible for having a wrong disposition, what am I held responsible for?" God holds each one responsible for not allowing Jesus Christ to deliver him from the wrong disposition when he sees that that is what He came to do. A man gets the seal of condemnation when he sees the light and prefers darkness (see John 3:19).

If you look upon Jesus Christ from the commonsense standpoint you will never discern who He is, but if you look upon Him as God manifested in the flesh for the purpose of putting the whole human race back to where God designed it to be, you get the meaning of redemption. The great, marvelous revelation of redemption is that it atones for everyone; people are "condemned to salvation" through the Cross of Christ. Discipleship is another matter. There are things to be brought about in this world that can only be done through those of us who are prepared to fulfill the conditions of discipleship. On the basis of the redemption I can, by committing myself to Jesus Christ and by receiving His Spirit as a gift, become a disciple in my actual life; that is, I can exhibit in my mortal flesh the life also of Jesus.

Man

What is man that You are mindful of him? (Psalm 8:4)

Man and Mankind

So God created man in His own image; in the image of God
He created him; male and female He created them.
(Genesis 1:27)

There is only one begotten son of God, one created son of God, and multitudes of regenerated sons of God through the redemption. These three stand in different categories.

The Bible speaks of only two men—Adam and Jesus Christ. *Mankind* is the term applied to the whole race of men, the mass of human beings. God did not make us in His own image; He made the federal head of the race in His image. "In the day that God created man, He made him in the likeness of God. He created them male and female, and blessed them and called them Mankind" (Genesis 5:1-2). Both man and woman are required for the completed creation of God. Jesus Christ is the last Adam in this sense, namely, that He reveals the characteristics of El Shaddai, the Father-Mother God, all vested in the unique manifestation of the Incarnation.

Man as He Was: "formed . . . of the dust of the ground" (Genesis 2:7)

> And the LORD God formed man of the dust of the ground, and breathed into his nostrils the breath of life. (Genesis 2:7)

Man as God created him is a revelation fact, not a fact we get at by our common sense. We have never seen Man. God created the earth and formed man of the dust of the ground, that is, God did not make man's body by a creative fiat, He deliberately built it out of the dust of created matter according to a design in the Divine mind. Adam and Jesus Christ both came direct from the hand of God. We are not creations of God. We are procreated through progenitors, the heredity of the human race is mixed; that accounts for all the perplexities. "And the LORD God formed man of the dust of the ground"—there is nothing the matter with matter; what has gone wrong is the infection of material things by sin, which is not material. Sin is not in matter and material things; if it were, it would be untrue to say that Jesus Christ, who was made in the likeness of men, was without sin.

Genesis 2:7 reveals that man's nature was a spiritual, sensuous nature—he was made of the dust of the ground, and God breathed into his nostrils the breath of life. These two things, dust and divinity, make up man. It is impossible for us to conceive what Adam was like before the Fall; his body must have been dazzling with light through his spiritual communion with God. When he took his rule over himself he not only lost his communion with God, lost the covering of glory and light inconceivable to us, but he also lost the dominion God intended him to have—"You have made him to have dominion over the works of Your hands": (Psalm 8:6). Men who are their own masters are masters of nothing else. A man may feel he ought to be master of the life in the sea and air and earth, but he can only be master on the line God designed he should, namely, that he recognize God's dominion over him. The only Being who ever walked this earth as God designed man was Jesus Christ. He was easily master of all created things because He maintained a steadfast obedience to the word and the will of His Father. "Who can this be, that even the winds and the sea obey Him?" (Matthew 8:27). Man's personal powers are apt to be looked at as a marvelous promise of what he is going to be; the Bible looks at man as a ruin of what he was designed to be. There have come down in humankind remnants, broken remnants, of the first creation; they are evidence of the magnificent structure God made in the beginning but not promises of what man is going to be.

Man as He Is: "by nature children of wrath" (Ephesians 2:3)

The words "you are of your father the devil" (John 8:44) were not addressed by Jesus to men generally, but to persistent religious disbelievers in Him.

The love of God and the wrath of God are obverse sides of the same thing, like two sides of a coin. The wrath of God is as positive as His love. God cannot be in agreement with sin. When a man is severed from God, the basis of his moral life is chaos and wrath not because God is angry, like a Moloch; rather it is His constitution of things. The wrath of God abides all the time a man persists in the way that leads away from God; the second he turns, he is faced with His love. Wrath is the dark line in God's face and is expressive of His hatred of sin. Civilization is the gloss over chaos and wrath. We are so sheltered that we are blinded to our need of God, and when calamity comes there is nothing to hold to. Over and over again in the history of the world people have made life into chaos. They try to find their true life in everything but God, but they cannot; they find the insistence of the Feet behind them all the time.

> But with unhurrying chase,
> And unperturbed pace,
> Deliberate speed, majestic instancy,
> They beat—and a Voice beat
> More instant than the Feet—
> "All things betray thee, who betrayest Me."
>
> Francis Thompson

Every love and justice and nobility in the world is loyal to Jesus Christ and only loyal to me when I recognize Him as their source. The Incarnation is the very heart of God manifested on the plane of chaos and wrath; what Jesus Christ went through in a time phase is indicated in such words as these: "My God, My God, why have You forsaken Me?" (Matthew 27:46). Jesus Christ came right straight down into the very depths of wrath, He clothed Himself with the humanity of the race that had fallen and could not lift itself, and in His own person He annihilated the wrath until there is no condemnation, no touch of the wrath of God, on those who are in Christ Jesus.

Man as He Will Be: "predestined to be conformed to the image of His Son" (Romans 8:29)

God's order is seen in the first and the last; the middle is the record of man's attempt to arrange things in his own way. Man is to be again in the image of God not by evolution, but by redemption. The meaning of redemption is not simply the regeneration of individuals, but that the whole human race is rehabilitated, put back to where God designed it to be; consequently any member of the human race can have the heredity of the Son of God put into him, namely, the Holy Spirit, by right of what Jesus did on the Cross. The task that confronted Jesus Christ was that He had to bring man, who is a sinner, back to God, forgive him his sin, and make him as holy as He is Himself;

and He did it single-handed. The revelation is that Jesus Christ, the last Adam, was made to be sin, the thing that severed man from God, and that He put away sin by the sacrifice of Himself—"that we might become the righteousness of God in Him" (2 Corinthians 5:21). He lifted the human race back not to where it was in the first Adam, but He lifted it back to where it never was, namely, to where He is Himself. "And it has not yet been revealed what we shall be, but we know that when He is revealed we shall be like Him, for we shall see Him as He is" (1 John 3:2).

Sin

Today the Bible revelation of sin as a positive thing has been revolted against, and sin is dealt with only as something that is ostensibly wrong. The Bible view is that there is something profoundly wrong at the basis of things. Sin is a revelation fact, not a commonsense fact. No natural man is ever bothered about sin; it is the saint, not the sinner, who knows what sin is. If you confuse *sin* with *sins,* you belittle the redemption, make it much ado about nothing. It is nonsense to talk about the need of redemption to enable a man to stop committing sins—his own willpower enables him to do that; a decent education will prevent him from breaking out into sinful acts, but to deny that there is a heredity of sin running straight through the human race aims a blasphemous blow at the redemption. The only word that expresses the enormity of sin is *Calvary.*

> Guilt remains guilt; you cannot bully God into any such
> blessing as turns guilt to merit, or penalty to rewards.
>
> Ibsen

Ibsen saw sin but not Calvary, not the Son of God as Redeemer. If it cost God Calvary to deal with sin, we have no business to make light of it.

God created Adam *innocent,* that is, he was intended to

develop not from evil to good, but from the natural to the spiritual by obedience. It was to be a natural progress. Adam switched off from God's design. Instead of maintaining his dependence on God he took his rule over himself and thereby introduced sin into the world. Sin is not wrong doing, it is wrong being, deliberate and emphatic independence of God. "Therefore, just as through one man sin entered the world, and thus death spread to all men, because all sinned" (Romans 5:12). It is not now a question of development. The problem is that an opposing force has come in that always says "I won't" and never can be made to say "I will." *I won't* is not the imperfect tense *I will*; it never develops into *I will*, its very nature is *shan't* and *won't*. Sin is mutiny against God's rule—not vileness of conduct, but red-handed anarchy. When you get sin revealed in you, you know that that phrase is not too strong. It is not that men are conscious anarchists—the devil is the only being in whom sin is conscious anarchy—but that a man perceives that that is the nature of sin once the light of God is thrown upon it. It is enmity against God, not *at* enmity, it *is* enmity. This opposing principle is abnormal. It was not in human nature as God designed it. The exposition of the nature of sin rarely enters into my human consciousness. When it does I know there is nothing in my spirit to deliver me from it, I am powerless; "sold under sin," wrote Paul. Jesus said, "Whoever commits sin is a slave of sin" (John 8:34).

Bear in mind that it requires the Holy Spirit to convict a man of sin. Any man knows that immorality is wrong, his conscience tells him it is; but it takes the Holy Spirit to convince a man that the thing he most highly esteems, that is, his own self-government, is an abomination in the sight of God. There is nothing more highly esteemed among men than self-realization, but it is the one thing of which Jesus Christ is the enemy because its central citadel is independence of God. If a man can stand on his own feet morally—and many a man can—what does he want with Jesus Christ and His salvation? with forgiveness? Some men are driven to God by appalling conviction of sins, but conviction of sins is not conviction of sin. Conviction of sin never comes as an elementary experience. If you try to convict a man of sin to begin with, you draw him to a plan of salvation but not to Jesus Christ.

The essence of sin is my claim to my right to myself. It goes deeper down than all the sins that ever were committed. Sin can't be forgiven because it is not an act; you can only be forgiven for the sins you commit, not for a heredity. "If we confess our sins, He is faithful and just to forgive us our sins" (1 John 1:9); sin must be cleansed by the miracle of God's grace. It does not awaken antipathy in a man when you tell him God will forgive him his sins because of what Jesus did on the Cross, but it does awaken antipathy when you tell him he has to give up his right to himself. Nothing is so much resented as the idea that I am not to be my own master. "If anyone desires to come after Me," said Jesus, "let him deny himself" (Matthew 16:24), that is, deny his right to himself, not merely give up external sins—those are exercrations. The point is, am I prepared deliberately to give up my right to myself to Jesus Christ? prepared to say, "Yes, take complete control"? If I am, Jesus Christ has gained a disciple. We don't go in for making disciples today, it takes too long; we are all for passionate evangelism—taken up with adding to the statistics of saved souls, adding to denominational membership—taken up with the things that show splendid quantifiable success. Jesus Christ took the long, long trail—"If anyone desires to come after Me, let him deny himself." Take time to make up your mind. People are not to be swept into the kingdom on tidal waves of evangelism, nor to have their wits paralyzed by supernatural means. They are to come deliberately, knowing what they are doing. One life straight through to God on the ground of discipleship is more satisfactory in His sight than multitudes who are saved but go no further. Over and over again men and women who should stand in the forefront for God are knocked clean out. When a crisis comes, the reason is not external wrongdoing, but something that has never been given up; there is something in which Jesus Christ has not had His right of way, and the discipleship is marred. God will give us ample opportunity of proving whether we have ever really given up the right to ourselves to Jesus Christ. The one who has offers no hindrance to the working of the Holy Spirit through him.

New Birth

As soon as we begin to examine the foundations of our salvation we are up against the thoughts of God, and as Christians we ought to be busy thinking God's thoughts after Him. That is where we fall short; we are delighted with the fact that once I was this, and now I am that, but simply to have a vivid experience is not sufficient if we are to be at our best for God. It is because of the refusal to think on Christian lines that Satan has come in as an angel of light and switched off multitudes of God's children in their heads, with the result that there is a divorce between heart and head. There is nothing simpler under heaven than to become a Christian, but after that it is not easy; we have to leave "the discussion of the elementary principles of Christ" and "go on to perfection" (Hebrews 6:1).

> Unless one is born again, he cannot see the kingdom
> of God. (John 3:3)

There is no natural law whereby a man can be born a second time—Nicodemus was right when he asked, "How can a man be born when he is old?" No one ought to need to be born again; the fact that he does indicates that something has gone wrong with the human race. According to modern thinking, man is a great being in the making; his attainments are looked on as a wonderful promise of what he is going to be. We are obsessed with the evolutionary idea. Jesus Christ talks about a revolution—"You must be born again" (John 3:7). The evolutionary idea doesn't cover all the facts. Not every person needs to be converted; *conversion* simply means turning in another direction—it may be a right or a wrong direction; but every individual needs to be born from above if he is ever going to see the kingdom of God. In listening to some presentations of the gospel you get the impression that a man has to be a blackguard before Jesus Christ can do anything for him. It is true that Jesus Christ can make a saint out of anyone, but the person down-and-out in sin is not the only class He deals with. It was to Nicodemus, a godly, upright man, not to a sinner as we understand the term, that He said, "Do not marvel that I said to you 'You must be born again.' " Count yourself in with the whole human race; it is necessary for you, the teacher of Israel, to be born again. It is easier to think about the sensational cases of men being transformed and lifted into a new realm by God's grace, but there are hundreds of men who are not sinners in the external sense. Does Jesus Christ do anything for them?

Many Christians don't seem to know what happened to them when they were born again. That is why they continually go back to the initial experience of having had their sins forgiven; they don't press on to full growth. In the New Testament new birth is always spoken of in terms of sanctification, not of salvation; to be *saved* means that a man receives the gift of eternal life, which is the gift of God; *sanctification* means that his spirit becomes the birthplace of the Son of God. "My little children, for whom I labor in birth again until Christ is formed in you" (Galatians 4:19). If Jesus Christ is going to be in me, He must come into me from the outside; He must be "formed" in me. It is not a question of being saved from hell, the redemption has to do with that; this is the redemption at work in my conscious life. I become a Bethlehem for the life of the Son of God. The duty of human nature is to sacrifice itself to nourish that life, and every now and again there are things demanded by the life of the Son of God in me that my human nature neither likes nor understands. What Simeon said to Mary, "A sword will pierce through your own soul also" (Luke 2:35), is true of my human nature. Am I willing for my human nature to be sacrificed in order that the life of the Son of God in me may be nourished, or do I only want Him to see me through certain difficulties? The way the life of the Son of God is nourished in me is by prayer and Bible revelation and by obedience when a crisis comes.

When I am born again my human nature is not different, it is the same as before; I am related to life in the same way, I have the same bodily organs, but the mainspring is different, and I have to see now that all my members are dominated by the new disposition (see Romans 6:13, 19). There is only one kind of human nature and that is the human nature we have all got, and there is only one kind of holiness, the holiness of Jesus Christ. Give Him elbow room, and He will manifest Himself in you, and other people will recognize Him. Human beings know human beings too well to mistake where goodness comes from; when they see certain characteristics they will know they come only from the indwelling of Jesus. It is not the manifestation of noble human traits, but of a real family likeness to Jesus. It is His gentleness, His patience, His purity—never mine. The whole art of spirituality is that my human nature should retire and let the new disposition have its way. We are told to follow His steps, but we can't do it; the heredity in us is not the same as it is in Jesus. Anyone who reads the Sermon on the Mount with his eyes open knows that something must happen if it is going to be lived out in him, for he has not the goods on board to produce the result. There is only one Being who can live the Sermon on the Mount and that is the Son of God. If I will walk in the light as God is in the light, then the holy nature of Jesus manifests itself in me. It is not that I receive an impartation of the Divine nature and then am left to work it out by myself—"Jesus Christ . . . became for us . . . sanctification" (1 Corinthians 1:30), that is, He is the holy nature that we receive.

"Blessed are the poor in spirit" (Matthew 5:3), said Jesus, because it is through that poverty I enter His kingdom; I cannot enter it as a good man or woman, I can only enter it as a complete pauper. The knowledge of my poverty brings me to the frontier where Jesus Christ works. As long as an individual is sufficient for himself, God can do nothing for him. Someone may be "paganly" all right, in fact a pagan is a delightful person to know, but he is not out at elbows, not troubled or upset, and he cannot understand why you should talk of the need to be born again. The born-again person has been put on the basis of a new construction of humanity, consequently for a time he is chaotic, disturbed, broken, and at this stage he is not so desirable as the person who represents the climax of the natural life. Other natural virtues are our deepest inheritance but when the miracle of new birth is experienced, the first thing that happens is the corruption of those virtues because they can never come anywhere near what God demands. Jesus Christ loved moral beauty (see Mark 10:21), but He never said it would do. The natural virtues are a delight to God because He designed them, they are fine and noble, but behind them is a disposition that may cause a person's morality to go by the board. What Jesus Christ does in new birth is to put in a disposition that transforms morality into holiness. He came to put into the person who knows he needs it His own heredity of holiness, to bring him into a oneness with God that he never had through natural birth, "that they may be one just as We are" (John 17:22).

The experimental aspect of redemption is repentance; the only proof that someone is born from above is that he brings forth "fruits worthy of repentance" (Matthew 3:8). That is the one characteristic of New Testament regeneration, and it hits desperately hard because the Holy Spirit brings conviction on the most humiliating lines. Many a powerless, fruitless Christian life is the result of a refusal to obey in some insignificant thing—"first go." It is extraordinary what we are brought up against when the Holy Spirit is at work in us, and the thing that fights longest against His demands is my prideful claim to my right to myself. The only sign of regeneration in practical experience is that we begin to make our lives in accordance with the demands of God.

Jesus Christ did not only come to present what God's normal man should be, He came to make the way for everyone of us to get there, and the gateway is His Cross. I cannot begin by imitating Jesus Christ, but only by being born into His kingdom; then when I have been regenerated and have received the heredity of the Son of God, I find that His teaching belongs to that heredity, not to my human nature.

All this means great deliberation on our part. God does not expect us to understand these things in order to be saved—salvation is of God's free grace—but He does expect us to do our bit in appreciation of "so great a salvation" (Hebrews 2:3).

Repentance

Never mistake remorse for repentance; remorse simply puts a man in hell while he is on earth. It carries no remedial quality with it at all, nothing that betters a man. An unawakened sinner knows no remorse, but as soon as a person recognizes his sin he experiences the pain of being gnawed by a sense of guilt for which punishment would be a heaven of relief, but no punishment can touch it. In the case of Cain (see Genesis 4:9–14) remorse is seen at its height: "My punishment is more than I can bear" (4:13). Cain was in the condition of being found out by his own sin; his conscience recognized what he had done, and he knew that God recognized it too. Remorse is not the recognition that I am detected by somebody else, I can defy that; remorse comes when, intellectually and morally, I recognize my own guilt. It is a desperate thing for me to realize that I am a sneak, that I am sensual and proud; that is my sin finding me out. The Holy Spirit never convicts of sin until He has got Jesus Christ pretty close up; a human being would like to convict of sin before Jesus Christ is there. The classic experience of Cain has all lesser experiences folded up in it; few of us are actually murderers, but we are all criminals in potentiality—"Whoever hates his brother is a murderer" (1 John 3:15); and one of the greatest humiliations in work for God is that we are never free from the reminder by the Holy Spirit of what we might be in actuality but for the grace of God.

When any sin is recalled with a gnawing sense of guilt, this biting again of remorse, watch carefully that it does not make you whine and indulge in sulks about the consequences. The beginning of sulks is blaming everybody but yourself, and every step you take in that direction leads further away from God and from the possibility of repentance. Whenever the lash of remorse comes, never try to prevent it; every bit of it is deserved. And if you are a worker, never tell a lie out of sympathy and say, "Oh, well, you don't need to feel like that, you couldn't help it." Never tell a lie to another soul. The temptation is tremendously strong to sympathize with a person and prove a traitor to his soul's true instincts; he may fling off from you at a tangent, but truth will tell in the end.

Reformation, which means "to form again" or "renew," is a law that works in human nature apart from the grace of God as well as after regeneration; if it takes place apart from regeneration it is simply the reformation of a rebel. Certain forms of wild oats bring forth their crop and pass and a person becomes different in conduct, but he is a deeply entrenched unregenerate person. That someone stops being bad and becomes good may have nothing to do with salvation; the only sign that an individual is saved is repentance. Instances of reformation apart from the grace of God can be multiplied because there is something in human nature that reacts toward reformation when the right influence is brought to bear at the right time, for example, the boy who won't reform for his father's threats or his schoolmaster's punishment will experience a reaction toward reformation through his mother's love. Again, though a bad man becomes worse in the presence of suspicious people, when with little children he experiences a reaction toward reformation. If being in the presence of a good man or woman does not produce a reaction toward goodness in me, I am in a bad way. The apostle Paul sums up this law when he says that "the goodness of God leads you to repentance" (Romans 2:4).

"Then Zacchaeus stood and said to the Lord, 'Look, Lord, I give half of my goods to the poor; and if I have taken anything from anyone by false accusation, I restore fourfold' " (Luke 19:8). Why did Zacchaeus say that? Who had said a word about his peculations! The desire to make restitution was stirred through his coming into the presence of Jesus and was a sign of the working of this inevitable law of reaction. *Restitution* means the determination to do right to everybody I have "done," and it is astonishing the things the Holy Spirit will remind us of that we have to put right. Over and over again during times of revival and great religious awakening workers are presented with this puzzle, that people do unquestionably make restitution—men who stole pay up like sheep, with no notion why they do it; if the worker is not well taught he will mistake this for the work of the Holy Spirit and a sign that they are born again, when the fact is that the truth has been so clearly put that it caused their nature to react towards reformation. The thing to do with people in that condition is to get them to receive something from God.

Luke 11:25 is a picture of clear, sweeping reformation, the house "swept and put in order" but what our Lord points out is the peril of a moral victory unused because the heart is left empty. The man who reforms without any knowledge of the grace of God is the subtlest infidel with regard to the need of regeneration. It is a good thing to have the heart swept, but it becomes the worst thing if the heart is left vacant for spirits more evil than itself to enter; Jesus said that "the last state of that man is worse than the first" (verse 26). Reformation is a good thing, but like every other good thing it is the enemy of the best. Regeneration means filling the heart with something positive, namely, the Holy Spirit.

Repentance is the experimental side of redemption and is altogether different from remorse or reformation. *Repentance* is a New Testament word and cannot be applied outside the New Testament. We all experience remorse, disgust with ourselves over the wrong we have done when we are found out by it, but the rarest miracle of God's grace is the sorrow that puts an end forever to the thing for which I am sorry. Repentance involves the receiving of a totally new disposition so that I never do the wrong thing again. The marvels of conviction of sin, of forgiveness, and of the holiness of God are so interwoven that the only forgiven person is the holy person. If God in forgiving me does not turn me into the standard of the Forgiver, to talk about being saved from hell and made right for heaven is a juggling trick to get rid of the responsibility of seeing that my life justifies God in forgiving me. The great element in practical Christianity—and that is the only kind of Christianity there is—is this note of repentance, which means I am willing to go all lengths so long as God's law that I have broken is cleared in my case, "that You may be found just when You speak, and blameless when You judge" (Psalm 51:4). Have I ever had a moment before God when I have said, "My God, I deserve all that You can bring on me as punishment for breaking Your holy law—'against You, You only, have I sinned, and done this evil in Your sight' "? The essence of repentance is that it destroys the lust of self-vindication; wherever that lust resides the repentance is not true. Repentance brings us to the place where we are willing to receive any punishment under heaven so long as the law we have broken is justified. That is repentance, and I think I am right in saying that very few of us know anything at all about it. We have the idea nowadays that God is so loving and gentle and kind that all we need do is to say we feel sorry for the wrong we have done and we will try to be better. That is not repentance. Repentance means that I am remade on a plane that justifies God in forgiving me.

Once get this kind of thing into your mind and you will understand what is meant by conviction of sin. The repentant man experiences the humiliating conviction that he has broken the law of God and he is willing to accept, on God's terms, the gift of a new life that will prove sufficient in him to enable him to live a holy life—not hereafter, but here and now. Strictly speaking, repentance is a gift of God; a man cannot repent when he chooses. Repentance does not spring out of the human heart, it springs from a ground outside the human heart: the ground of the redemption.

Reality

The Will to Believe the Redeemer

> Blessed are those who have not seen and yet have believed. (John 20:29; cf. John 11:40)

Reality is the thing that works out absolutely solidly true in my personal life, but I must be careful not to confound the reality of my experience with reality itself. For instance, when I am born again I am not conscious of the redemption of my Lord, the one thing that is real to me is that I have been born again; but if I watch the working of the Holy Spirit I find that He takes me clean out of myself till I no longer pay any attention to my experiences. I am concerned only with the reality that produced those experiences, namely, the redemption. If I am left with my experiences, they have not been produced by the redemption. If experience is made the only guide it will produce that peculiar type of isolated life that is never found in the New Testament.

We say seeing is believing, but it is not; we must believe a thing is possible before we would believe it even though we saw it. Belief must be the will to believe, and I can never will to believe without a violent effort on my part to dissociate myself from all my old ways of looking at things and putting myself right over on to God. It is God who draws me, my relationship is to Him; consequently the issue of will comes in at once: will I transact on what God says? Never discuss with anyone when God speaks; discussion on spiritual matters is impertinent. God never discusses with anyone. Let me stake my all, blindly as far as feelings are concerned, on the reality of the redemption, and before long that reality will begin to tell in my actual life, which will be the evidence that the transaction has taken place. But there must be the deliberate surrender of will, not a surrender to the persuasive power of a personality, but a deliberate launching forth on God and what He says. Remember, you must urge the will to an issue; you must come to the point where you will to believe the Redeemer and deliberately wash your hands of the consequences.

In testing for ourselves our relation to reality we are not left in a vague fog. We have the Word of God expressing God to us, and the Word of God, our Lord Jesus Christ, expresses Himself to us through His teaching made vitally applicable to every domain of human life. Any attempt to divorce the words of God from the Word of God leads to unreality; the words of God are only vitally real when we are in a right relationship to God through the Word. Men worship an intellectual creed, and you can't dispute it because it is logically correct, but it does not produce saints. It produces stalwarts and stoics but not New Testament saints, because it is based on adherence to the literal words rather than on a vital relationship to God, who is the one abiding reality. In the final issue Christian principles are found to be antichrist, meaning, an authority other than Christ Himself. It is quite possible to have an intellectual appreciation of the redemption without any experience of supernatural grace; an experience of supernatural grace comes by committing myself to a person, not to a creed or a conviction. I can never find reality by looking within; the only way I can get at reality is by dumping myself outside myself on to Someone else, namely, God. As soon as I do I am brought in touch with reality.

The Will to Receive the Redeemer.

But as many as received Him (John 1:12)

We do not create truth, we receive it. There are things that you perceive clearly, but are they real to you? They are not real if you have never been through a transaction of will in connection with them. Your perception is based on the weaving of your own brain, not on the knowledge of Someone who knows you. The Giver is God, and every gift He offers is based on His knowledge of us; our attitude is to be that of receiving from Him all the time, and in this way we become sons and daughters of God. It requires the greatest effort and produces the greatest humility to receive anything from God; we would much sooner earn it. Receiving is the evidence of a disciple of the Lord; reasoning about it is the indication of a dictator to God. Effective repentance is witnessed by my receiving from God instead of reasoning why God should give to me. When I am willing to be such a fool as to accept, that is repentance; the other is rational pride. We can only get at reality by means of the conscience, which ultimately embraces both head and heart. There is always a practical proof when we do get at reality: actuality is made in accord with it. Does your intellect make you in accord actually with what you think? Of course it does not. Read the lives of some of the most intellectual men, men whose aesthetic sensibilities are of the finest order, but their actual lives won't bear looking at. I cannot get at reality by my intellect or by emotion, but only by my conscience bringing me in touch with the redemption. When the Holy Spirit gets hold of my conscience He convicts me of unreality, and when I respond to God I come in touch with reality and experience a sense of wonder—"That He should have done this for me!" It is not extravagant, it is the result of a totally new adjustment, a relation to the reality that has been created in me by means of my abandonment to Jesus Christ.

The Will to Obey the Redeemer.

> If you love Me, keep My commandments. (John 14:15; 21, 23; 15:11–12)

These verses are specimens of many that reveal what is to be the abiding attitude of the saint, namely obeying the commandments of One whom we can only believe by will and whose gifts we can only receive by will. We will to believe Him, then we obey by will. These exercises of the will are essential to the wholesome upkeep of a saint's actual life. The effort on the human side is to maintain the childlike relation to God, receiving from Him all the time, then obedience works out in every detail. When a person is rightly related to God it is the Holy Spirit who works through him, and as long as he maintains the will to believe, the will to receive, and the will to obey, the life of Jesus is manifested in his mortal flesh.

Beware of any hesitation to abandon to God. It is the meanest characteristics of our personalities that are at work whenever we hesitate; there is some element of self-interest that won't submit to God. When we do cut the shore lines and launch forth, what happens is a great deal more than a vision of the indwelling of God; what happens is the positive miracle of the redemption at work in us, and we have patiently to make it permeate everything. Our relationship to God is first that of personality, not of intellect; intellect comes in after to explain what has transpired, and it is the ordering of the mind that makes a man a teacher and an instructor. Be stably rooted in God and then begin to know, begin to use those rusty brains.

Beware of having an overweening interest in your own character so that you are inclined to believe in God on that account; at the same time, be careful to allow nothing that would hinder your relationship to God because any impairing of that relationship hinders Him in getting at other souls through you. Continually revise your relationship to God until the only certainty you have is not that you are faithful, but that He is. Priggishness is based on concern for my own whiteness, a pathetic whine—"I'm afraid I'm not faithful; I'm afraid I shall never be what God wants me to be." Get into contact with reality and what you feel no longer matters to you because the one terrific reality is God.

An abiding way of maintaining our relation to reality is

intercession. Intercession means that I strive earnestly to have my human soul moved by the attitude of my Lord to the particular person I am praying for. That is where our work lies, and we shirk it by becoming active workers; we do the things that can be tabulated and scheduled, and we won't do the one thing that has no snares. Intercession keeps the relationship to God completely open. You cannot intercede if you do not believe in the reality of redemption; you will turn intercession into futile sympathy with human beings that only increases their submissive content to being out of touch with God. Intercession means getting the mind of Christ about the one for whom we pray; that is what it means to "fill up in my flesh what is lacking in the afflictions of Christ" (Colossians 1:24); that is why there are so few intercessors. Be careful not to enmesh yourself in more difficulties than God has engineered for you to know; if you know too much, more than God has engineered, you cannot pray; the condition of the people is so crushing that you can't get through to reality. The true intercessor is the one who realizes Paul's meaning when he says, "For we do not know what we should pray for as we ought, but the Spirit Himself makes intercession for us with groanings which cannot be uttered" (Romans 8:26).

The Holy Spirit

The Holy Spirit and Revelation Purpose.

> Holy men of God spoke as they were moved by the Holy
> Spirit. (2 Peter 1:21)

Bear in mind that there is a two-fold attitude to be maintained in dealing with the self-revelation of God: first, its historic setting; second, its value to me personally. It is essential to have a historic basis for our Christian faith; our faith must be centered in the life and death of the historic Jesus. Why is it that that life and death have an importance out of all proportion to every other historic fact? Because there the redemption is brought to a focus. Jesus Christ was not a Man who, twenty centuries ago, lived on this earth for thirty-three years and was crucified; He was God Incarnate, manifested at one point in history. All history prior looked forward to that point; all history since looks back to it. The presentation of this fact produces what no other fact in the whole of history could ever produce—the miracle of God at work in human souls. The death of Jesus was not the death of a martyr, it was the revelation of the eternal heart of God. That is why the Cross is God's last word; that does not mean God is not speaking still, it means that He is saying nothing contrary to the Cross.

The tendency abroad today is to do away with the historic setting of the revelation of God in Christ in the Gospels, to do away with what the apostles wrote, and to say, "All that is needed is to receive the Holy Spirit and we will have a private interpretation of our own." But "no prophecy of Scripture is of any private interpretation, for prophecy never came by the will of man, but holy men of God spoke as they were moved by the Holy Spirit" (verses 20-21). That makes it incumbent upon us to be reverent to a degree with what the apostles wrote. The Epistles are not the cogitations of men of extraordinary spiritual genius, but the posthumous work of the ascended Christ and they have therefore a peculiar significance in the program of redemption. The Holy Spirit used these men, with all their personal idiosyncrasies, to convey God's message of salvation to the world. Our Lord, so to speak, incarnated Himself in them—the message of God must always be incarnated but it remains the message of God. The Epistles are the exposition of why God became manifest in the flesh, and when by submissive reception I commit myself to that revelation, the Holy Spirit begins to interpret to me what Jesus Christ did on the Cross.

"I do not pray for these alone, but also for them who will believe in Me through their word" (John 17:20). Everyone who believes on Jesus believes on Him "through their word." In the experience of salvation all are alike; in the matter of authoritative inspiration the apostles stand alone; their word is as final as Jesus Christ's. We have no counterpart to that. The inspiration the Holy Spirit gives us is not for revelation purposes, but for insight into the revelation already given. Apostolic inspiration is not an experience, it is as great a miracle as the Incarnation. The one great need is for the Holy Spirit to be received because He will open up to us not only our own salvation and the whole of the New Testament revelation, He will open up the treasures of the Old Testament—"the mystery which has been hidden from ages and from generations, but now has been revealed to His saints. . . . which is Christ in you, the hope of glory" (Colossians 1:26–27).

The Holy Spirit and Redemptive Preaching.

> For the message of the cross is foolishness to those who are perishing. . . . it pleased God through the foolishness of the message preached to save those who believe. (1 Corinthians 1:18, 21)

We are nowhere told to preach salvation or sanctification or divine healing; we are told to lift up Jesus who is the Redeemer, and He will produce His redemptive results in the souls of men. If I preach only the effects of the redemption, describe in persuasive speech what God has done for me, nothing will happen. It is only when I am humble enough and stupid enough to preach the Cross that the miracle of God takes place. The preaching of the Cross creates that which enables a man to believe in God because the Cross is the manifestation of the redemption. The Cross condemns men to salvation. The foolishness of preaching is the way God has chosen to make the redemption efficacious in human lives. You can't persuade a man to believe in God. Belief in God is not an act of the intellect; it is a moral creation produced by the interaction of God's Spirit and my spirit in willing obedience. Intellect comes in afterward to explain what has happened. In preaching the Cross we use our intellect not to prove that Jesus died, but to present the fact of His death. The danger is to give expression to subjective experiences we have had but that will never produce the same experiences in others; it is personal testimony and has its right place, but it is not preaching the Cross. The bedrock, permanent thing in Christian experience is not the accidental bits of God's particular manifestation of it in you and me, the bedrock, permanent thing is the redemption, our particular experiences of it, slight or profound, are simply meant to introduce us to that reality.

The Holy Spirit and Revealing Power.

> However, when He, the Spirit of truth, has come, He will guide you into all truth. . . . He will glorify Me. (John 16:13–14)

If an expositor has never realized the need to receive, recognize, and rely on the Holy Spirit, he takes little account of the Cross but says, "Let us come to the teachings of Jesus." Our Lord never placed the emphasis on what He taught, neither do the apostles; they place all the emphasis on the Cross. Why? because they were shrewd and intelligent? no, because the Holy Spirit inspired them to put the emphasis there. "But God forbid that I should boast except in the cross of our Lord Jesus Christ" (Galatians 6:14). Our Lord is not the great Teacher of the world; He is the Savior of the world and the Teacher of those who believe in Him, which is a radically different matter. His teaching is of no use except to agonize mankind with its ideals, unattainable until men are made anew through the Cross. Unless I am born from above the only result of the teachings of Jesus is to produce despair. People say that Jesus Christ came to teach us to be good; He never did! All the teaching in the world about a man having a pure heart won't make it pure. Our Lord's teaching has no power in it unless I possess His nature. When I am born from above it is the conscientious relationship between my individual life and Jesus Christ that keeps my conduct right. Once I am brought into contact with reality I begin to experience the power of the redemption as it applies to every phase of life.

> For He will take of what is Mine, and declare it to you.
> (John 16:14)

The spirit of antichrist is that spirit which dissolves by analysis the person of Jesus—someone unique, but not what the New Testament claims. To preach the Jesus of the Gospels at the expense of the Christ of the Epistles is a false thing, such a false thing that it is antichrist to the very core because it is a blow direct at what Jesus said the Holy Spirit would do, namely, expound Him to the disciples and, through their word, to innumerable lives to the end of time. If I say, "Of course God would never convey a right interpretation of Himself through a handful of men like the disciples," I am casting a slur on what Jesus said, telling Him that His reliance on God's promise of the Spirit was without justification, that His basis of confidence on the Holy Spirit's revelation of Him to the disciples was misplaced. When our Lord told the disciples they would do greater works, His reliance was not on them, but on the gift of the Spirit that He was to receive from the Father and shed forth on them. Everything Jesus said the Holy Spirit would do, He has done, and the New Testament is the revelation of it.

The Holy Spirit and Revealed Proclamation.

> He Himself gave some to be apostles . . . for the edifying of
> the body of Christ. (Ephesians 4:11–12)

Our Lord gave the disciples the gift of the Holy Spirit as their equipment for proclaiming the gospel to the world; in the same way the Holy Spirit comes into my personal life to bring me out of my individual narrowness into the universal purpose of God. When I want to translate all God's redemptive work into the consciousness of being saved, I become a pious humbug. God does not save me in order that I may feel saved, but to take me up into His redemptive purpose. Christian experience must be expounded as it emerges in its most extraordinary and tragic form, not in order to make that form the standard, but as giving the basis to which every experience is to be traced. You say, "I have never had such profound conviction of sin, such depth of repentance, as the apostle Paul, therefore I can't be a true Christian." We are not meant to imitate Paul in his experience, but to remember that that profound experience gives us the right direction for tracing where our own experience comes from. Paul never says, "Follow my way of getting into Christ," because no two people ever come the same way into Christ, yet they must follow the same ways in Christ. Experience is simply the doorway into reality. If I stick in the doorway I get cold and die, die away from reality; I must go through the doorway and in the classic experiences we get the door widest open.

The New Testament is the product of the Holy Spirit; we are literally fed into the body of Christ by its words. "Feed My sheep" (John 21:17), said Jesus, and all down the ages the words of the New Testament have fed the children of God; if we try to nourish ourselves in any other way we produce abortions, what the writer to the Hebrews calls "bastards" (Hebrews 12:8 KJV). The point for me is not simply that I appreciate with my mind what the New Testament declares, but that I am brought into such a relationship with God that His words become serviceable through me to others. It sounds pathetic to talk about drawing on the life of Jesus to keep the needs of my physical life supplied; that is not His meaning. It is drawing on the life of Jesus through His Word that He might serve out nourishment to others through me.

Natural and Personal Life

Never run away with the idea that you are a person who has a spirit, has a soul, and has a body; you are a person that is spirit, soul, and body. Man is one; *body, soul* and *spirit* are terms of definition. My body is the manifest me. Some of us are so dominated by the body that our own spirit lives only in the physical domain instead of the physical being slowly taken into the spiritual by a series of moral choices. The spirit goes no further than we bring the body. One of the best means of spiritual progress is to learn to deny the body in a great number of unnecessary ways (cf. 1 Corinthians 9:27).

First Corinthians 15:46 ("However, the spiritual is not first, but the natural; and afterward the spiritual") lays down the fundamental basis of the way God deals with man all through—first the natural, then the spiritual. The whole purpose of a human personality is to turn the natural life into a spiritual life by sacrifice. The Bible never speaks of the natural life as sinful; it contrasts it with the spiritual, for example, "the natural man does not receive the things of the Spirit of God . . . nor can he know them because they are spiritually discerned. But he who is spiritual judges all things" (1 Corinthians 2:14–15).

Adam, the federal head of the human race, was designed by God to take part in his own development, that is, he was intended to turn the natural into the spiritual by a series of choices that would mean moral progress. The natural life is the lamb for sacrifice. It is not fanaticism, but the sacrificing of what is absolutely legitimate and right and making it spiritual by obedience. That is the only way personality is exhibited in its true form. It has nothing to do with sin; there would have been sacrifice whether there had been sin or not because of God's design of man. It was not a sin for our Lord to have a human body, it was not a sin for Him to eat, but it would have been sin for Him to eat during the forty days in the wilderness because His Father's will was otherwise. Our Lord stands as the presentation of God's normal man, and when by regeneration His life is formed in us we have to transform the natural life into a spiritual life by obedience to the will of God, letting Him engineer our circumstances as He will. We are not fundamentally free, external circumstances are not in our hands, they are in God's hands; the one thing in which we are free is in our personal relationship to God. We are not responsible for the circumstances we are in, but we are responsible for the way we allow those circumstances to affect us; we can either allow them to get on top of us or we can allow them to transform us into what God wants us to be. If we go under in circumstances we are held responsible because God has promised an absolutely overcoming Spirit to any man who will receive Him. If you are at a loss to know how to get at what God wants you to be, listen to the Lord Jesus. It's as though He said, "If you ask God He will plant in you the very Spirit that is in Me" (see Luke 11:13). If you receive the Holy Spirit you find that circumstances will never have power to do anything but give you the chance of sacrificing the natural to the spiritual and proving you are a son or daughter of God.

"And the LORD God . . . breathed into his nostrils the breath of life" (Genesis 2:7), God breathed into man that which became man's spirit, that which is the indestructible factor in every human being. Man is, and he will never be uncreated. Man has kinship with God as no other creation of God has; his true kinship is with God and nowhere else. When I receive the Holy Spirit He lifts my personality back into its primal relationship with God. The Holy Spirit coming into my spirit never becomes my spirit; He energizes my spirit and enables me "both to will and to do for His good pleasure" (Philippians 2:13).

God has put man in an experimental sphere and if he refuses to turn the natural into the spiritual he will find himself dominated by the body; it will chain him down and make him a slave. The personality of a person apart from the Spirit of God becomes enslaved to the desires of the flesh. The marvel of the life of God in a person is that he never need be dominated by anything other than spirit: "Walk in the Spirit, and you shall not fulfill the lust of the flesh" (Galatians 5:16). But if you don't sacrifice your natural inclinations and impulses to the will and the Word of God, you are likely to be tripped up by any of the things Paul mentions: "Now the works of the flesh are evident, which are . . ." (verse 19). It will test a man to the limit to take his stand on the redemption and on the indwelling of the Holy Spirit and to prove in actual life what God has put in him by regeneration. We are taken up with the soul-saving line instead of the line of character building on the basis of the redemption; consequently you get people who are gloriously saved but they have never gone on to sacrifice the natural to the spiritual—have never put the knife to the throat of an appetite, have never recognized pigheaded obstinacy, have never got on the track of that green-eyed monster, envy. "But those things can't be in me now that I am saved"—and they are painted in glaring colors! When the Holy Spirit begins to unearth the works of the flesh in you, don't temporize, don't whitewash them; don't call suspicion discernment of the spirit or ill-temper righteous indignation; bring it to the light, come face to face with it, confess it, and get it cleansed away.

"And those who are Christ's have crucified the flesh with its passions and desires" (verse 24). When a man is saved his human nature is not altered; human nature is marred by sin but it is not bad. Deliverance from sin does not mean deliverance from human nature. By regeneration a man is perfectly adjusted to God; now he is required to do a man's bit, namely, to take his human nature and make it serve the new disposition. The honor of Jesus Christ is at stake in my bodily life, and if I walk in the Spirit I will be ruthless to the things that won't submit to Him. To crucify the flesh with its passions and desires is not God's business, it is man's.

"And afterward the spiritual" (1 Corinthians 15:46). We are made partakers of the Divine nature through the promises (see 2 Peter 1:4); the inherent tendency of the Divine nature is implanted in us through regeneration and we become children of God; we become, that is, not only what we are by nature, creations of God, but sons and daughters of God with a strong family likeness to Jesus. The true conception of Man is our Lord. Man got out of God's order, and we are brought back not merely into the original order, but into a much better position through our Lord, namely, we are to be conformed to the image of His Son. We look at the things that are expressed externally; God looks at the tendency born in us. He knows, apart from all our pious phrases and pretenses, whether we have been regenerated. He sees what the life will become. Browning puts it as no other writer outside the Bible:

> All I could never be,
> All, men ignored in me.
> —This, I was worth to God.

Discovering God

Evangelical v. Eclectic Expression

> The effort is on an individual and philanthropic scale, not on a world scale, an evangelical scale—it is unequal to the world crisis. . . . It is the climax of a generation of genial and gentle religion, with the nerve of the Cross cut, which therefore breaks in our hands at a great historic crisis for lack of the moral note—tonic, radical, and redemptive.
>
> Forsyth

Evangelical: the belief that God was manifested in the flesh in the person of His Son in order that through His death on the Cross men might be redeemed. The apostle Paul sums up evangelical belief when he says: "For He made Him who knew no sin to be sin for us, that we might become the righteousness of God in Him" (2 Corinthians 5:21); that is, Jesus Christ takes my heredity of sin and gives me His own heredity of holiness, and I show the alteration through my skin. The emphasis is apt to be put on one phase only: justification by faith; the real center of the action of the redemption has to do with a man's ruling disposition. If a man takes the rational commonsense line, he despises the evangelical view, but when he gets down to things as they are he finds that the rational view is on the fifteenth story and the evangelical view is at the basis. The rational view misses the fact that there is a hiatus between God and man; things are wild, there is a tragedy, something irrational—not rational—at the heart of life, and the way out is not by reason, but only through the Cross of Christ. These things are fundamental, they come straight home to the problems of a man's own heart and life. The point for me is, do I agree with God in what He condemns in the Cross? That is where most of our Christianity is proved to be humbug. We believe in what we call the plan of salvation, but we don't do much else. We ought to be busy thinking as Christians. Up to the time of the war, religious people were taken up not so much with the fundamental revelation of the redemption as with expounding a certain type of saintliness, a particular presentation of the Gospel; consequently when the war struck they were not able to grasp the providential order of God at all, they were found enervated, unequal to the world crisis.

Temperamental v. True Portrayal

> God so loved, so unsparingly, as to do His Son's body and soul the injury of the Cross. That is the principle on which God's love dealt with the vast evil of the world. He reserved for Himself what He forbade Abraham to do.
>
> Forsyth

Temperament: the way a person looks at life. My temperament is an inner disposition that influences my thoughts and actions to a certain extent, that is, I am either pessimistic or optimistic according to the way my blood circulates. It is an insult to take the temperamental line in dealing with a human being, "Cheer up, look on the bright side"; there are some types of suffering before which the only thing you can do is to keep your mouth shut. There are times when a person needs to be handled by God, not by his fellow man, and part of the gift of human wisdom is to know how to be reverent with what he does not understand.

To take the temperamental view of Jesus Christ will mean that I do not make the revelation of the Bible my guide. I portray Him as one who lived beyond His age and suffered in consequence; all He did was to leave us a good example that we must try to follow so that when a man makes the supreme sacrifice and lays down his life, he thereby redeems his own soul. A more hopeless misunderstanding of the redemption could not be. When a person lays down his life, it takes God to expound what has occurred. "Greater love has no one than this, than to lay down one's life for his friends" (John 15:13). The love of God is seen in that He laid down His life for His enemies. The redemption is God's "bit." "None of them can by any means redeem his brother, nor give to God a ransom for him—for the redemption of their souls is costly, and it shall cease forever" (Psalm 49:7–8).

What Forsyth is pointing out is that the temperamental view ignores the fact that God deliberately paid the price of dealing with sin. It is easy, if I reason from the logical, commonsense point of view, to say that God created the man who became a sinner and then condemns him to hell because he sinned. The Bible says nothing of the sort. The Bible says that God Himself accepted the responsibility for sin; the Cross is the proof that He did. It cost Jesus Christ to His last living drop of blood to deal with "the vast evil of the world." The true portrayal is that the Cross is not the cross of a man, but the Cross of God. The tragedy of the Cross is the hurt to God. In the Cross, God and sinful man merge; consequently the Cross is of more importance than all the world's civilizations.

"He who did not spare His own Son, but delivered Him up for us all, how shall He not with Him also freely give us all things?" (Romans 8:32). What does that mean? It means that I can receive a new disposition the second I see my need: "If you then, being evil, know how to give good gifts to your children, how much more will your heavenly Father give the

Holy Spirit to those who ask Him!" (Luke 11:13). It is so simple that the majority of us blunder over it; we won't come the childlike way; but when a person is up against the wall the words of Jesus become the deepest philosophy in life: "Come to Me" (Matthew 11:28); "Believe also in Me" (John 14:1) My relation to things proves whether or not I do believe in Jesus. The life of a child of God is always the life of a child, simple and openhearted, no ulterior motive. The Bible makes more of the death of Jesus than of His life and His teaching because the teaching of Jesus does not apply to you and me unless we have received His Spirit. What is the good of telling me to love my enemies? I hate them! to be fathomlessly pure in heart? to have no unworthy motive? The teaching of Jesus is for the life He puts in, and I receive that life by means of the Cross.

Dogmatic Creed v. Deity of Christ

No man begins his Christian life by believing a creed. The person with a dogmatic creed says, "You must believe this and that." Jesus says, in effect, "Do the will," that is, commit yourself to Me. Truth is not in a particular statement; Truth is a person: "I am . . . the Truth" (John 14:6). It is a mistake to attempt to define what a man must believe before he can be a Christian; his beliefs are the effect of his being a Christian, not the cause of it. As soon as you lose sight of the central, majestic figure of Jesus Christ you are swept off your feet by all kinds of doctrine, and when big things hit, you find your religion does not stand you in good stead because your creed does not agree with the Truth.

The revelation of the deity of Christ does not come first to a man's intellect, but to his heart and life, and he says with amazement, "You are the Christ, the Son of the living God" (Matthew 16:16). The great point of the Bible revelation of God is not only that God was in Christ, but that Jesus Christ is God. If Jesus Christ is not God, then the only God we have is an abstraction of our own minds. I know no other God in time or in eternity than Jesus Christ; I have accepted all I know of God on the authority of the revelation He gave of Him. "He who has seen Me has seen the Father." (John 14:9).

We never discover God until we come to a personal need for Him, and that drives us to Jesus. The whole meaning of life is that a man discovers God for himself. It is not sin that keeps us away from Jesus, but our own goodness. "I did not come to call the righteous," Jesus said, "but sinners, to repentance" (Matthew 9:13). We don't seem to need God until we come up against things. The basis for thinking with most of us is our ordinary, logical common sense, but when a man comes up against things he has to go deeper down than his common sense, to fall back on something else, either fatalism or God. The Christian thought is not fatalistic, it is based on the revelation of God given by Jesus Christ.

Common Christian Thinking

The Divine Unction of Christian Teaching

> But you have an anointing from the Holy One, and you know all things. (1 John 2:20)

The apostle John, in these verses, does away with the idea that there are specialists in Christian thinking as there are specialists in other domains; he says, "No, the Holy Spirit is the one Teacher, and the teaching He imparts is common to us all; consequently there is no excuse for any of us, no room for saying, "I haven't had a good education," or, "I haven't had time to study." The majority of us recognize the necessity of receiving the Holy Spirit for living, but we do not sufficiently recognize the need for drawing on the resources of the Holy Spirit for thinking. Many of us don't realize that we can think; we lie all abroad in our minds, woolgathering. When we receive the Holy Spirit He imparts the ability to see things by intuition. Spiritual intuition lives in the same sphere as natural intuition plus the Holy Spirit.

> *I do not like thee, Dr. Fell,*
> *The reason why I cannot tell;*
> *But this I know, and know full well—*
> *I do not like thee, Dr. Fell.*

That is natural intuition: instant perception of the truth of things without reasoning or analysis. Instruction in spiritual intuition is what we need. The Holy Spirit will curb and check natural intuition until He brings it into accord with what Jesus meant when He said, "My sheep hear My voice" (John 10:26). When you listen to a preacher, how are you going to know whether he is teaching the truth of God? Only by spiritual intuition. You may know that God has wonderfully used a man in the past, but never make that your ground for heeding what he says now, for at any minute a man may be out of touch with God (cf. 1 Corinthians 9:27). Never pin your faith to a man's reputation as a servant of God, always watch for the Holy Spirit. If a man is talking the truth of God, those who listen will meet it again whether they like it or not; if he is not talking God's truth, they won't come across it anymore. Whenever the grand, simple sanity of the Holy Spirit's interpretation is wanting, hold the matter in abeyance. The one stamp of the right interpretation is its warm natural sanity; it is not fantastic or peculiar, it doesn't twist your brain. It makes you feel, "How marvelously simple and beautiful that is!"

The Holy Spirit's anointing abides "in you," says John (see 1 John 2:27). At the beginning of your spiritual life you wanted to run off to this teacher and that, to this book and that, until you learn that the anointing abides in you. John and Paul and Peter all insist on the superb right of the humblest believer to test the teacher by the anointing that is in him. If we put teachers over against the Holy Spirit, when God removes them we go down, we mourn and say, "What shall we do now?" Watch how Paul deals with the people who say, " 'I am of Paul,' or 'I am of Apollos,' or 'I am of Cephas' " (1 Corinthians 1:12); he says in effect, All teachers are yours. A teacher is simply meant to rouse us up to face the truths revealed in the Bible and witnessed to by the Holy Spirit. Watch the tendency that is in us all to try to safeguard God's truth. The remarkable thing is that God never safeguards His own truth; He leaves statements in the Scriptures that we can easily misrepresent; the only test is the Holy Spirit who leads us into all truth.

"And you do not need that anyone teach you" (1 John 2:27). It is here that Satan comes in as an angel of light and says, in effect, "If you are anointed by the Spirit, everything you think is right." Not at all. Only as we obey the Spirit and keep in the light does the anointing abide. Our thinking and commonsense reasoning must be rigorously subordinated to the Spirit, and if we abide true to Him He repairs the damage sin has done to conscience and mind and keeps our thinking vital and true. Notice in your own life how He works. He begins with the big, general principles and then slowly educates you down to the scruple.

The Divine Union of Christian Thinking.

> But as the same anointing teaches you concerning all things.
> (1 John 2:27)

We have perennially to rely on the one great source of all teaching, the Holy Spirit; He puts us in an independent position toward all other teachers and makes our dependence on Himself as the one Teacher the only basis of union there is, "the unity of the Spirit. . . .There is one body and one Spirit . . . one Lord, one faith, one baptism" (Ephesians 4:3–5). "Be filled with the Spirit," says Paul (Ephesians 5:18). Most of us have seen the seashore, when the tide is out, with all its separate pools; how are those pools to be made one? by digging channels between them? No. Wait till the tide comes in, and where are the pools? Absolutely lost, merged in one tremendous floodtide. That is exactly what happens when Christians are indwelt by the Holy Spirit. Let people be filled with the Holy Spirit and you have the ideal of what the New Testament means by the church. The church is a separated band of people who are united to God by the regenerating power of the Spirit, and the bedrock of membership in the church is that we know who Jesus is by a personal revelation of Him. The indwelling Spirit is the supreme Guide, and He keeps us absorbed with our Lord. The emphasis today is placed on the furtherance of an organization; the motto is, "We must keep this thing going." If we are in God's order the thing will go; if we are not in His order, it won't. Think of the works that are kept on after God wanted to rule them out of the way because they have a source of inspiration apart from Him.

"You will abide in Him" (1 John 2:27). The test that we are being taught by the Holy Spirit is that our lives are proving identical with the life of the Son of God. You cannot have identity without individuality. False teaching says we lose our personalities; we never do. Jesus Christ emancipates personality, and He makes individuality pronounced, but it is personality absolutely free from my right to myself, free from identity with any other personality, manifesting a strong family likeness to Jesus, and the transfiguring element is love to Him.

The Psychology of Faith I

The Constitution of Faith

Without faith it is impossible to please Him. (Hebrews 11:6)

There is not possible a normal healthy human being apart from religious faith. Faith claims the whole man and all God's grace can make him.

Forsyth

The conception of faith given in the New Testament is that it must embrace the whole man. Faith is not a faculty, faith is the whole man rightly related to God by the power of the Spirit of Jesus. We are apt to apply faith to certain domains of our lives only—we have faith in God when we ask Him to save us or ask Him for the Holy Spirit, but we trust something other than God in the actual details of our lives. "Faith claims the whole man and all that God's grace can make him," just as it claimed the whole of our Lord's life. Our Lord represents the normal man, not the average man, but the man according to God's norm. His life was not cut up into compartments, one part sacred and another secular; it was not in any way a mutilated life. Jesus Christ was concentrated on one line, namely, the will of His Father, in every detail of His life. That is the normal standard for each of us, and the miracle of the gospel is that He can put us into the condition where we can grow into the same image. Our Lord lived His life not in order to show how good He was, but to give us the normal standard for our lives. The life He lived is made ours by means of His death; by the gift of the Holy Spirit and obedience to Him, we are put into the relationship to God that Jesus had—"that they may be one as We are" (John 17:11).

Faith is a tremendously active principle of trust in Jesus that is ready to venture on every word He speaks: "Lord, You have said, for example, 'Seek first the kingdom of God and His righteousness, and all these things shall be added to you' (Matthew 6:33)—it looks mad, but I am going to venture on it; I will sink or swim on Your word." We cannot have faith in every word of Jesus whenever we think we will. The Holy Spirit brings a word of Jesus to our remembrance and applies it to the circumstances we are in. The point is, will we obey that particular word? We may have seen Jesus and known His power and yet never have ventured out in faith on Him. Faith must be tested because only through conflict can head faith be turned into a personal possession. Faith according to Jesus must have its object real, no one can worship an ideal. We cannot have faith in God unless we know Him in Jesus Christ. God is a mere abstraction to our outlook until we see Him in Jesus and hear Him say, "He who has seen Me has seen the Father" (John 14:9), then we have something to build upon and faith becomes boundless.

Faith and Confusing Issues

> Thus also faith by itself, if it does not have works, is dead.
> (James 2:17)

> An inadequate theory of faith distorts practice.
> Forsyth

The apostle James persistently exhorts us saying, in effect, "If you have faith, prove it by your life." Experience is never the ground of my faith; experience is the evidence of my faith. Many of us have had a marvelous experience of deliverance from sin and of the baptism of the Holy Spirit—not a fictional experience, but a real experience whereby we prove, to our amazement every day, that God has delivered us. Then comes the danger that we pin our faith to our experience instead of to Jesus Christ, and if we do, faith becomes distorted. When the baptism of the Holy Spirit came upon the early disciples it made them the written epistles of what they taught, and it is to be the same with us. Our experience is the proof that our faith is right. Jesus Christ is always infinitely mightier than our faith, mightier than our experience, but our experience will be along the line of the faith we have in Him. Have we faith to bear this testimony to those who know us—that we are what we are because of our faith in Jesus? We have faith in Jesus to save us, but do we prove that He has saved us by living a new life? I say I believe that Jesus can do this and that; well, has He done it? "But by the grace of God I am what I am" (1 Corinthians 15:10). Are we monuments of the grace of God, or do we only experience God's supernatural power in our work for Him? Extraordinary spiritual experiences spring from something wrong in the life. You never get the exquisite, simple faith in God along any special line of experience, but only along the common line of regeneration through faith in Jesus. Be skeptical of any revelation that has not got as its source the simplicity by means of which a "babe" can enter in and which a "fool" can express.

Faith and Consecrated Issues

Work out your own salvation. (Philippians 2:12)

The normal course of all religious experience is expansion followed by concentration.

Forsyth

When God gives a vision of what sanctification means or what the life of faith means, we have instantly to pay for the vision, and we pay for it by the inevitable law that "expansion must be followed by concentration." That means we must concentrate on the vision until it becomes real. Over and over again the vision is mistaken for the reality. God's great, divine anticipation can only be made manifest by our human participation; these two must not be put asunder. Every expansion of brain and heart that God gives in meetings or in private reading of the Bible must be paid for inevitably and inexorably by concentration on our part, not by consecration. God will continually bring us into circumstances to make us prove whether we will work out with determined concentration what He has worked in. If you have had a vivid religious experience of the baptism of the Holy Spirit, what are you going to do with it? We are sanctified by God's grace and made one with Jesus in order that we might sanctify our holiness to God as Jesus did. "And for their sakes I sanctify Myself" (John 17:19). There is no difficulty in getting sanctified if my will and affections have at the heart the earnest desire for God's glory. If I am willing for God to strangle in me the thing that makes me everlastingly hanker after my own point of view, my own interests, my own whitewashed purity—if I am willing for all that to be put to death, then the God of peace will sanctify me wholly. (see 1 Thessalonians 5:23). Sanctification means a radical and absolute identification with Jesus until the springs of His life are the springs of my life. "Faith is He who calls you is faithful, who also will do it" (verse 24).

The great need today is for Christians to toe the line: " 'And the nations shall know that I am the LORD,' says the Lord GOD, *'when I am hallowed in you before their eyes'* " (Ezekiel 36:23, italics added). Unless Christians are facing up to God's commands there is no use pushing forward to meet the life of our time. Jesus wants us to face the life of our time in the power of the Holy Spirit. Do we proclaim by our lives, by our thinking, by our faith in God that Jesus Christ is sufficient for every problem life can present? that there is no force too great for Him to cope with and overcome? If our faith is not living and active it is because we need reviving; we have a faith that is limited by certain doctrines instead of being the faith of God.

The apostle Paul is always tremendously practical, he comes right down to where we live; he says we must work out the salvation God has worked in. "All authority has been given to Me" (Matthew 28:18), said Jesus, and by the Holy Spirit's presence we can do those things that please God—are we doing them? By the power of the indwelling Holy Spirit we can bring every thought and imagination into captivity to the obedience of Christ and can keep this body the chaste temple of the Holy Spirit—are we doing it? By the power of the Holy Spirit we can keep our communications with other people the exact expression of what God is working in us—are we doing it? The proof that we have a healthy, vigorous faith is that we are expressing it in our lives and bearing testimony with our lips as to how it came about.

There is no end to the life of faith; sanctification itself is only the ABC of the Christian life. The life of Jesus from Bethlehem onward is a picture of the sanctified life, and anything that would make our souls stagnate produces a distortion. It is a continual learning, but not of the same lesson. If we have to be taught the same lesson it is because we have been very stupid. God will bring us into circumstances and make us learn the particular lessons He wants us to learn and, slowly and surely, we will work out all that He works in. There is no patience equal to the patience of God.

The Psychology of Faith II

Faith and the Son of God

> . . . looking unto Jesus, the author and finisher of our
> faith. (Hebrews 12:2)

> He fought the battle, He proved the possibility of victory,
> He showed us the place and revealed to us the secret of the
> power.
>
> Forsyth

Jesus Christ is the Captain of our faith; He has gained the victory; consequently, for us Satan is a conquered foe. When we are sanctified and have become His brethren we are put, not in the place of the first Adam, but in the place of the last Adam, where we live by the power and might of the faith of the Son of God. We have to get rid of the idea that because Jesus was God He could not be tempted. Almighty God cannot be tempted, but in Jesus Christ we deal with God as man, a unique Being—God-Man. It was as Son of Man that "He fought the battle, He proved the possibility of victory." After His baptism, Satan, by the direct permission of the Holy Spirit, tested the faith of Jesus ("Immediately the Spirit drove Him into the wilderness" Mark 1:12). Satan broke what Adam held straight off; but he could not break what Jesus held in His person though he tested Him in every conceivable way; therefore having Himself suffered, being tempted, "He is able to aid those who are tempted" (Hebrews 2:18).

When we are born again we get our introduction into what God calls temptation. When we are sanctified we are not delivered from temptation, we are loosened into it; we are not free enough before, either morally or spiritually, to be tempted. A soon as we become His brethren we are free, and all these subtleties are at work. God does not shield any man or woman from any requirements of a full-grown man or woman. Luke 22:28 ("But you are those who have continued with Me in My trials") presents our Lord's view of His life as Man; a life of temptations, not triumphs. When we are born again the Son of God is submitted to temptations in our individual lives; are we remaining loyal to Him in His temptations in us? When temptation comes, stand absolutely true to God no matter what it costs you, and you will find the onslaught leaves you with affinities higher and purer than ever before. Temptation overcome is the transfiguration of the natural into the spiritual and the establishment of conscious affinity with the purest and best.

Faith and the Sons of God

Beloved, now we are children of God. (1 John 3:2)

Having been made sons of God does not absolve us from the lifelong task of actually making ourselves sons of God.

Forsyth

We have to take pains to make ourselves what God has taken pains to make us. You can take a horse to the trough, but you can't make him drink; you can send your child to school, but you can't make him study; God can put a saint into a right relationship with Himself, but He cannot make him work out that relationship. The saint must do that himself. We must take the pains to make ourselves visibly all that God has made us invisibly. God alters our dispositions, but He does not make our characters. When God alters my disposition the first thing the new disposition will do is to stir up my brain to think along God's line. As I begin to think, begin to work out what God has worked in, it will become character. Character is consolidated thought. God makes me pure in heart; I must make myself pure in conduct. This point of working things out in actuality is apt to be lost sight of.

The business of faith is to convert truth into reality. What do you really believe? Take time and catalog it up; are you converting your belief into reality? You say, "I believe God has sanctified me." Does your actual life prove He has? "I believe God has baptized me with the Holy Spirit." Why? because you had cold shivers and visions and marvelous times of prayer? The proof that we are baptized with the Holy Spirit is that we bear a strong family likeness to Jesus, and men take knowledge of us, as they did of the disciples after Pentecost, that we have been with Jesus. They recognize the family likeness at once. True justification can only result in sanctification. By justification God anticipates that we are holy in His sight, and if we will obey the Holy Spirit we will prove in actual life that God is justified in justifying us. Ask yourself, "Is God justified in my justification? Do I prove by the way I live and talk and do my work that God has made me holy? Am I converting God's purpose in justifying me into actual experience or only delighting in God's anticipation?"

There is a great snare, especially in evangelical circles, of knowing the will of God as expressed in the Bible without the slightest practical working of it out in the life. The Christian religion is the most practical thing on earth. If the Holy Spirit has given you a vision, in your private Bible study or during a meeting, that made your heart glow and your mind expand and your will stir itself to grasp, you will have to pay to the last farthing in concentration along that line until all you saw in vision is made actual. During these past years there has been a terrific expansion in lives through bereavement and sorrow; everything in individual life has been altered, but there is the price to pay. The price is the same in national as in individual life.

The peculiar aspect of religious faith is that it is faith in a person who relates us to Him and commits us to His point of view, it is not faith in a point of view divorced from relationship to a person. If you would know My doctrine, said Jesus, do My will (see John 7:17). Our Lord never teaches first by principles, but by personal relationship to Him. When through His redemption we become rightly related to Him personally, our hearts are unshakably confident in Him. That is the divine anticipation being participated in, the tremendous work of God's supernatural grace being manifested in our mortal flesh.

The Psychology of Faith III

Mental Belief

> But as many as received Him, to them He gave the right to
> become children of God, to those who believe on His name.
> (John 1:12)

John 1:12–13 is a grand, mighty, all-embracing word—*to as
many as received Him.* The way mental belief works is that it leads
us to understand who Jesus Christ is and what He can do for us
and in us. Jesus Christ is the normal Man, the Man according to
God's standard, and God demands of us the very holiness He
exhibited.

A spiritually minded Christian has to go through the throes
of a total mental readjustment; it is a God-glorifying process, if a
humbling one. People continually say, "How can I have more
faith?" You may ask for faith to further orders, but you will never
have faith apart from Jesus Christ. You can't pump up faith out of
your own heart. Whenever faith is starved in your soul it is
because you are not in contact with Jesus; get in contact with
Him and lack of faith will go in two seconds. Whenever Jesus
Christ came across people who were free from the curse of
finality that comes from religious beliefs, He awakened faith in
them at once. The only ones who were without faith in Him were
those who were bound up by religious certitude. Faith means that
I commit myself to Jesus, project myself absolutely on to Him,
sink or swim—and you do both—you sink out of yourself and
swim into Him. Faith is implicit confidence in Jesus and in His

faith. It is one thing to have faith in Jesus and another thing to have faith about everything for which He has faith. Galatians 2:20 does not refer to the apostle Paul's elementary faith in Jesus as his Savior, but to the faith of Jesus. He says that the identical faith that was in Jesus Christ, the faith that governed His life, the faith that Satan could not break, is now in him through identification with the death of Jesus; the faith that characterized Him now characterizes Paul.

Moral Belief

> Knowing this, that our old man was crucified with Him, that the body of sin might be done away with, that we should no longer be slaves of sin. (Romans 6:6)

If we are honest and obedient, moral belief will follow mental belief very quickly. Am I poor enough, humble enough, and simple enough to believe in Jesus? Do I believe Him when He says that God will give me the Holy Spirit if I ask Him? If I do believe in Jesus and receive the Holy Spirit on the authority of His Word, then I will have to make a moral decision about all that the Holy Spirit reveals. He will reveal to me what sin is, and He will reveal that Jesus Christ can deliver me from sin if I will agree with God's verdict on it in the Cross. Many of us do believe in Jesus, we have received the Holy Spirit and know we are children of God, and yet we won't make the moral decision about sin, namely, that it must be killed right out of us. It is the great moment of our lives when we decide that sin must die right out, not be curbed or suppressed or counteracted, but crucified. It is not done easily; it is only done by a moral wrench. We never understand the relation between a human life and the Cross of Christ until we perform a moral act and have the light of God thrown upon reality.

The transactions that tell in my life for God are moral decisions, not mental ones. I may think through everything there is in Christian doctrine and yet remain exactly the same; but I never make a moral decision and remain the same, and it is the moral decisions to which the Holy Spirit is always leading us on the basis of the redemption. A moral decision is not a decision that takes time—one second is sufficient; what takes time is my stubborn refusal to come to the point of morally deciding. Here, where we sit, we can decide whether or not the redemption shall take its full course in us. Once I decide that it shall, the great inrush of the redemption takes effect immediately. There are times when the Holy Spirit does touch us, times when there are "flashes struck from midnight" and we see everything clearly, and that is where the danger comes in because we are apt to let those touches pass off in sentimental ardor instead of making a moral decision. It is a sensible delight to feel God so near, but unless a moral decision is made you will find it much harder next time to pay attention to the touch when it comes. It is better to decide without the accompaniment of the glow and the thrill—better to decide in cold blood, when your own will is in the ascendant, deliberately swayed by the rulership of Christ.

Mystic Belief

> For you died, and your life is hidden with Christ in God.
> (Colossians 3:3)

Paul is not talking to disembodied spirits, he is talking to men and women who have been through identification with the death of Jesus and know that their "old man" is crucified with Him. If we are born again of the Holy Spirit and have made the moral decision to obey what He reveals about sin, then we must go on to believe that God can enable us to live for His glory in any circumstances He places us in. You can always detect the right kind of belief in Jesus by a flesh-and-blood testimony. "Therefore by their fruits you will know them" (Matthew 7:20). Other people are not likely to confuse grapes with thorns or figs with thistles. Mystic belief means that we enter into a conscious inheritance of what the redemption has wrought for us and daily, hourly, manifest the marvel of the grace of God in our actual lives.

The majority of us hang on to Jesus Christ, we are thankful for the massive gift of salvation, but we don't do anything toward working it out. That is the difficult bit and is also the bit the majority of us fall in, because we have not been taught that that is what we have to do. Consequently, there is a gap between our religious profession and our actual practical living. To put it down to human frailty is a wiggle. There is only one word for it, and that is *humbug*.

In my actual life I live below the belief that I profess. We can do nothing toward our salvation, but we can work out what God works in, and the emphasis all through the New Testament is that God gives us sufficient energy to do it if we will. The great factor in Christian experience is the one our Lord continually brought out, namely, the reception of the Holy Spirit who does in us what He did for us, and slowly and surely our natural lives are transformed into spiritual lives through obedience.

Notes On Lamentations

The Lamentations are not the expression of the grief of a disappointed man. The peculiar element in Jeremiah's sorrow is that he is identifying himself with an unrepentant people (cf. Daniel 9:4–20). We suffer on account of our own wrong or the wrong of others, but that is not vicarious suffering. Jeremiah's grief personifies vicariously the grief of the whole nation. Am I prepared to be a scapegoat for the sins of others for which they are still unrepentant?

← = mournful, melancholy, plaintive poem

Elegy in Degradation: Chapter 1

> How lonely sits the city that was full of people! . . . She weeps bitterly in the night, her tears are on her cheeks. (1:1–2)

The city herself is introduced weeping and giving expression to her sorrow over the evil determined against her on account of her sins.

"How lonely sits the city." Being alone is not loneliness; loneliness has in it an element of moral disesteem: "Jerusalem has sinned gravely, therefore she has become vile. All who honored her despise her" (verse 8). Cain's solitude is typical of this loneliness; so is the loneliness of the prodigal son in the far country, who starved on what the pigs throve on. Man was not created to be alone. Jesus Christ was rarely alone; the times when He was alone are distinctly stated. Solitude, to be beneficial, must never be sought and must never be on account of sin. If I choose solitude, I go back into active life with annoyance and a contempt for other people, proving that my seeking solitude was selfish.

"He has spread a net for my feet" (verse 13). There is no choice after the choice is made. We are at the mercy of God's inexorable justice once the choice is made that leads into the net. Our destiny is not determined for us, but it is determined by us. Man's free will is part of God's sovereign will. We have freedom to take which course we choose but not freedom to determine the end of that choice. God makes clear what He desires, we must choose, and the result of the choice is not the inevitability of law, but the inevitability of God. Verse 18 gives the reason for all that is happening: "The LORD is righteous, for I rebelled against His commandment." God will never change His character to please people's pleading or petulance if they have deliberately spurned His counsel.

There are irreparable losses in human life, and no amount of whining will alter it. The Garden of Eden was closed, not to naughty children, but to sinners and is never again opened to sinners. The way of the tree of life is guarded, preventing man getting back as a sinner; he only gets back, and thank God he does get back, in and through the redemption. What is prophesied with regard to Jerusalem is the attitude of the Spirit of God to the human race. The attitude of those not indwelt by the Spirit of God is that man's capabilities are a promise of what he is going to be, the Holy Spirit sees man as a ruin of what he once was. He does not delight in his natural virtues. We are being told what a splendid race of human beings we are! We are a race of rebels, and the rebellion has got to be destroyed. When the Holy Spirit is having His way with a man the first thing He does is to corrupt confidence in that which belongs to a ruin. Nothing is more highly esteemed among men than pride in their virtues, that is, self-realization, but Jesus Christ said that "what is highly esteemed among men is an abomination in the sight of God" (Luke 16:15). If this was realized we would understand the extravagant language of Scripture about sin.

Elegy in Destruction: Chapter 2

> How the Lord has covered the daughter of Zion with a
> cloud in His anger! He cast down from heaven to the earth
> the beauty of Israel. (2:1)

The prophets of God have always one burden when they deal with the judgments of God and that is that they come not from the east nor from the west but are directly stamped as from the Lord. The tendency today is to put the consequences of sin as natural consequences; the consequences of sin have a righteous God behind them. We take the Bible idea out of punishment and say, "Oh, well, it is the inevitable result"; the Bible says the inevitable result is brought about by a personal God. "The Lord was like an enemy" (verse 5). Deliverance comes through destruction, and for a while the soul does not know whether God is a friend or an enemy. God has one purpose in destruction and that is the deliverance of His own. God's own is not you, but His own in you. All that is saved is the work of God in a man, nothing else. Destruction means the obliteration of every characteristic of the life that is not rooted in godliness, it never means the annihilation of the life. The judgments of God are a consuming fire whereby He destroys in order to deliver; the time to be alarmed in life is when all things are undisturbed. The knowledge that God is a consuming fire is the greatest comfort to the saint. It is His love at work on those characteristics that are not true to godliness. The saint who is near to God knows no burning, but the farther away from God the sinner gets, the more the fire of God burns him.

In verses 1–9, the wrath of God is emphasized. God's love is wrath toward wrong; He is never tender to that which hates goodness. All through, the Bible reveals that when communion with God is severed the basis of life is chaos and wrath. The chaotic elements may not show themselves at once, but they will presently. All that this Book says about corruption in connection

66   *Conformed to His Image*

with the flesh is as certain as God is on His throne if the life is not rightly related to God. When we speak of the wrath of God, we must not picture Him as an angry sultan on the throne of heaven bringing a lash about people when they do what He does not want. There is no element of personal vindictiveness in God. It is rather that God's constitution of things is such that when a man becomes severed from God his life tumbles into turmoil and confusion, into agony and distress; it is hell at once, and he will never get out of it unless he turns to God. As soon as he turns, chaos is turned into cosmos, wrath into love, distress into peace. "Knowing, therefore, the terror of the Lord" (2 Corinthians 5:11), we persuade men to keep in touch with Him. The world pays no attention to those who tell how God convicted of sin and how He delivered them; the warnings of God are of no use to sinners until they are convicted of sin and the warnings become applicable to them.

"The elders of the daughter of Zion sit on the ground and keep silence" (Lamentations 2:10). When God's destructions are abroad there is no power to move, only to sit; no power to speak, only to keep silence. It is not a time for social intercourse of any kind, but for the deepest dejection.

"My eyes fail with tears . . . because of the destruction of the daughter of my people" (verse 11). No prophet stands so close to Jesus Christ as Jeremiah; he is the one who realizes human conditions more keenly than any other and identifies himself with them. Verses 11–19 are thus lamentation over the impotence of human consolation.

"Your prophets . . . have not uncovered your iniquity" (verse 14). The prophet with a message based on human morality excuses sin instead of detecting it: "God knows you can't help this sort of thing"—that is a lie. Falsely, he adds, "Under the circumstances you will be excused." Jeremiah was indignant with those prophets who gave a wrong application to God's message: "Sin is sin, but you don't need to imagine that that is the reason for what God is doing"; Jeremiah held that it was the reason.

"... the day of the Lord's anger" (verse 22). When God's limit is reached, He destroys into salvation; He destroys the unsaveable and liberates the saveable. Judgment days are an overflowing mercy because they separate between right and wrong. To be experimental in me the salvation of Jesus Christ is always a judgment, and it brings the understanding of God's justice even in His severest judgments. If we compare our attitudes with the revelations made in God's Book we find how despicably shallow we are. The attitude is not one of sympathy of God, not a sensitive understanding of His point of view, only an amazing sensitivity over our own calamities and those of other people. Consequently, we act on the principle of giving a pill to cure an earthquake. When God is squeezing the life of a man or of a nation in order to save the remnant, what is the use of my coming and kicking at the fingers of God and saying, "I shan't allow You to do this"? If our human sympathy with the one who is suffering under the hand of God is justified, then God is cruel. Some of us are so set on our own honor that we have no time for God's honor.

"Is this the city that is called 'the perfection of beauty, the joy of the whole earth'?" (verse 15). Jeremiah is referring to the desolation that by God's own decree, has fallen on everything God made to be holy; he sees God's judgment on His own choicest things—Jerusalem ruined, the temple destroyed. "See, O LORD, and consider! To whom have You done this?" (verse 20). And Jeremiah's whole heart was in Jerusalem! God did not spare His people. His judgment on them was as unconquerably certain as it was on Babylon and as it is on us. No amount of pleading will ever alter the judgments of God.

Elegy in Desolation: Chapter 3

> Surely He has turned His hand against me time and time again throughout the day. (3:3)

Obedience to God will mean that some time or other you enter into desolation; if you don't obey, you won't—for a time.

Jeremiah is speaking in vicarious terms of the sorrow and anguish of the people under God's chastisement; he is not cutting a cross-section through his own personal grief, not writing his own spiritual autobiography. Jeremiah is a vicarious sufferer, that is, he does not find his place in other people, he lets other people find their place in him. Our attitude too often is, "Oh, that has nothing to do with me, I have enough to bear." We will be of no use in God's service until that spirit is removed. God so loves the world that He hates the wrong in it. Do I so love men and women that I hate the wrong in them? Most of us love other people for what they are to us instead of for what God wants them to be. The distress worked in a man's heart by the Holy Spirit is never on his own account, but always on God's account.

> Desperate tides of the whole great world's anguish
> Forced thro' the channels of a single heart.

Have I ever shared for a moment God's concern over people, or am I putting myself in a bandage before God and saying, "I can't stand any more"?

"Why should a living man complain, a man for the punishment of his sins?" (verse 39). The judgments of God leave scars, and the scars remain until I humbly and joyfully recognize that the judgments are deserved and that God is justified in them. The last delusion God delivers us from is the idea that we don't deserve what we get. When we see ourselves under the canopy of God's overflowing mercy we are dissolved in wonder, love, and praise. That is the meaning of repentance, which is the greatest gift God ever gives a man. As long as my heart has never been broken by conviction of sin, I don't understand the psalmist when he says, "The sacrifices of God are a broken spirit, a broken and a contrite heart—these, O God, You will not despise" (Psalm 51:17). When you get there God is the only reality; but you only get there through heartbreak and sorrow. Holiness is based on repentance, and the holy man is the most humble man you can meet. My realization of God can be measured by my humility. Jeremiah's reliance on the justice of God breaks into a prayer in which is manifested his confidence that God will send help—"I called on Your name, O LORD, from the lowest pit. You have heard my voice: 'Do not hide Your ear from my sighing, from my cry for help' " (verses 55–56).

Elegy in Dispersion: Chapter 4

> When they fled and wandered, those among the nations said, "They shall no more sojourn here." (verse 15).

"How the gold has become dim! How changed the fine gold!" (verse 1). It is the holiest things that are desolated. God ordained the temple, Jerusalem was His holy city, and yet He allows them to be ruined. Flesh and blood, man's body, is meant to be the temple of the Holy Spirit—God's "gold," but sin renders it disreputable. The depth of possible sin is measured by the height of possible holiness. When men come under conviction of sin by the Holy Spirit their "beauty is consumed away, like as it were a moth fretting a garment." The misery that conviction brings enables a man to realize what God created him for, namely, to glorify God and to enjoy Him forever. *= gross wickedness, sin*

"The punishment of the iniquity of the daughter of my people is greater than the punishment of the sin of Sodom, which was overthrown in a moment" (verse 6). The destruction of Sodom was a sudden calamity; the destruction of Jerusalem was a terribly long, heartrending depreciation of everything of value in God's sight.

"[It is] because of the sins of her prophets and the iniquities of her priests, who shed in her midst the blood of the just" (verse 13). Beware of iniquity, which means conjuring yourself out of the straight, finding reasons why you did not do what you know you should have done. The term *iniquity* is used only of the people of God. To shed just blood refers to more than actual murder. The

Bible never deals with proportionate sin; according to the Bible an impure thought is as bad as adultery, a covetous thought is as bad as a theft. It takes a long education in the things of God before we believe that is true. Never trust innocence when it is contradicted by the Word of God. The tiniest bit of sin is an indication of the vast corruption that is in the human heart ("For from within, out of the heart of men, proceed . . ." Mark 7:21–23). That is why we must keep in the light all the time. Never allow horror at crime to blind you to the fact that it is human nature like your own that committed it. A saint is never horror-struck because, although he knows that what our Lord says about the human heart is true, he knows also of a Savior who can save to the uttermost.

"Your iniquity is accomplished" (verse 22). My guilt is ended when I repent, when I stop admitting and begin confessing. Am I blaming any of my forebears for my present condition? Then my punishment will go on till I blame them no more. Am I blaming the circumstances in which I live? Then my punishment will go on till I stop blaming my circumstances. As long as I have any remnant of an idea that I can be cleared in any other way than by God through the redemption, my punishment will go on. The instant I stop blaming everything but myself and acquit God of injustice to me, my recognition of Him begins.

Elegy in Devotion: Chapter 5

> Remember, O LORD, what has come upon us; look and behold our reproach! (verse 1)

What had Jeremiah done to deserve in the tiniest degree all that has come upon him? nothing but obey God in every detail, and because of his obedience he was in the midst of the distress. The one man who has kept unspottedly right with God is in all the desolation, realizing it more keenly than any of those who deserved it. A snare spiritually is to refuse to carry about "in the body the dying of the Lord Jesus" (2 Corinthians 4:10), and prefer the happy hilarity that is only possible for long in the new heaven and new earth. We are here for one purpose: to "fill up in my flesh what is lacking in the afflictions of Christ" (Colossians 1:24)—spoiled for this age, alive to nothing but Jesus Christ's point of view. In this order of things it is a maimed life, and few of us will have it; we prefer a full-orbed life of infinite satisfaction that makes us absolutely crass to what is happening in "Jerusalem." We can never be marked by the angel as those who sigh and cry for the sorrows of Jerusalem.

"Our fathers sinned and are no more, but we bear their iniquities" (Lamentations 5:7). These words are not to be understood as intimating that the speakers conceived themselves innocent—"Woe to us, for we have sinned!" (verse 16). The sins of the fathers are not visited on innocent children, but on children who continue the sins of their fathers (see Exodus 20:5; Ezekiel 18:1–9). Distinction must be made between *punishment* and *suffering;* they are not synonymous terms. A bad man's relation to his children is in God's hand; a child's relation to the badness of his father is in his own hand. Because we see children suffering physically for the sins of their parents we say they are being punished; they are not. There is no element of punishment in their suffering; there are divine compensations we know nothing about. The whole subject of heredity and what is transmitted by heredity, if taken out of its Bible setting, can be made the greatest slander against God as well as the greatest exoneration of the bitterness of a man's spirit.

"The crown has fallen from our head. . . . Because of this our heart is faint; because of these things our eyes grow dim" (verses 16–17). These words convey the poignancy of penitence. Nothing will make a man's heart cave in and his eyes stop seeing, except sin. Sorrow won't do it, misfortune won't do it, hardship won't do it; on the contrary these things, if there is no sin, make a man's heart strong. The *fallen crown* is the figurative expression for the honorable position of the people of God that they have now lost. Sin may make a man more desirable in the eyes of the world—"the sin which so easily ensnares us" (Hebrews 12:1), but what makes a man ugly physically, morally, and spiritually is the discovery of sin by his own heart, and all attempts to justify himself spring from the depth of conviction of private sin.

The gathering in of God's salvation around a man means that he is checked at first by the merest zephyr touch—there is nothing so gentle as the check of the Holy Spirit. If he obeys, emancipation is at once; if he does not obey, the zephyr touch will turn into a destructive blow from which there is no escape. There is never any shattering blow of God on the life that pays attention to the checks of the Spirit, but every time there is a spurning of the still small voice, the hardening of the life away from God goes on until destruction comes and shatters it. When I realize that there is something between God and me, it is at the peril of my soul I don't stop everything and get it put right. As soon as a thing makes itself conscious to me, it has no business there.

To sum up the Lamentations: the words of this vicarious sufferer direct the grieving human heart, in its deep sorrow, to the only true Comfort.

Duty of the Heart

Then one of the scribes . . . asked Him, "Which is the first commandment of all?" (Mark 12:28)

In answering the scribe's question our Lord does not say anything original. He takes two commandments from their place in the Old Testament where they are obscured (see Deuteronomy 6:5, Leviticus 19:18) and brings them out into a startling light. "Do not think," He said, "that I came to destroy the Law or the Prophets. I did not come to destroy but to fulfill" (Matthew 5:17).

Duty of Love for God.

"And you shall love the LORD your God with all your heart, with all your soul, with all your mind, and with all your strength." This is the first commandment. (Mark 12:30)

Deut. 6 : 5

Where do we find ourselves with regard to this first great duty, "You shall love the LORD your God with all your heart"? What does that phrase mean to us? If Jesus had said, "You shall love your lover with all your heart," we would have known what He meant. Well, He did mean that, but the Lover is to be God. The majority of us have an ethereal, unpractical, bloodless abstraction that we call love for God; to Jesus love for God meant the most passionate, intense love of which a human being is capable.

The writer to the Hebrews states that Jesus Christ was made "perfect through sufferings," (Hebrews 2:10) but there is any amount of suffering that "im-perfects" us because it springs from unregulated passions. This fact has made some ethical teachers say that the passions themselves are evil, something human nature suffers from. Our Lord teaches that the passions are to be regulated by this first duty of love for God. The way we are to overcome the world, the flesh, and the devil is by the force of our love for God regulating all our passions until every force of body, soul, and spirit is devoted to this first great duty. This is the one sign of sanctification in a life; any experience of sanctification that is less than that has something diseased about it.

If my first duty is to love God, the practical, sensible question to ask is, "What is God like?" Aristotle taught that love for God does not exist; "it is absurd to talk of such a thing, for God is an unknown being." The apostle Paul met with the result of his teaching in his day:

> "Men of Athens, . . . as I was passing through and considering the objects of your worship, I even found an altar with this inscription:
> TO THE UNKNOWN GOD.
> Therefore, the One whom you worship without knowing, Him I proclaim to you." (Acts 17:22–23).

Today the teaching in many of our own colleges and universities is being honeycombed with pagan philosophy, pagan ethics; consequently there is a state of mind produced that appreciates what Aristotle said, that we cannot know God. Then what a startling statement Jesus made when He said, "You shall love the LORD your God with all your heart!"

"No one has seen God at any time. The only begotten Son, who is in the bosom of the Father, He has declared Him (John 1:18). Jesus knew God, and He makes Him known: "He who has seen Me has seen the Father" (John 14:9). Get into the habit of recalling to your mind what Jesus was like when He was here; picture what He did and what He said, recall His gentleness and tenderness as well as His strength and sternness, and then say, "That is what God is like." I do not think it would be difficult for us to love Jesus if He went in and out among us as in the days of His flesh, healing the sick and diseased, restoring the distracted, putting right those who were wrong, reclaiming backsliders—I do not think it would be difficult for us to love Him. That is to love God. The great Lover of God is the Holy Spirit, and when we receive the Holy Spirit we find we have a God whom we can know and whom we can love with all our hearts because we see "the light of the knowledge of the glory of God in the face of Jesus Christ" (2 Corinthians 4:6).

Duty of Love to Man

> And the second, like it, is this: "You shall love your neighbor as yourself." (Mark 12:31)

Lev. 19:18

Everything our Lord taught about the duty of man to man might be summed up in the one law of giving. It is as if He set Himself to contradict the natural counsel of the human heart, which is to acquire and keep. A child will say of a gift, "Is it my own?" When a man is born again that instinct is replaced by another, the instinct of giving The law of the life of a disciple is give, give, give (see Luke 6:38). As Christians our giving is to be proportionate to all we have received of the infinite giving of God. "Freely you have received, freely give" (Matthew 10:8). Not how much we give, but what we do not give is the test of our Christianity. When we speak of giving we nearly always think only of money.

Money is the lifeblood of most of us. We have a remarkable trick—when we give money we don't give sympathy, and when we give sympathy we don't give money. The only way we get insight into the meaning for ourselves of what Jesus taught is by being indwelt by the Holy Spirit because He enables us, first of all, to understand our Lord's life; unless we do that, we will exploit His teaching, take out of it only what we agree with. There is one aspect of giving we think little about but which had a prominent place in our Lord's life, namely, that of social interaction. He accepted hospitality on the right hand and on the left, from publicans and from the Pharisees, so much so that they said He was "a glutton and a winebibber, a friend of tax collectors and sinners!" (Luke 7:34). He spent Himself with one lodestar all the time, to seek and to save that which was lost. And Paul says, "I have become all things to all men, that I might by all means save some" (1 Corinthians 9:22). How few of us ever think of giving socially! We are so parsimonious that we won't spend a thing in conversation unless it is on a line that helps us!

And who is my neighbor? (Luke 10:29). Jesus gives an amazing reply, namely that the answer to the question, "Who is my neighbor?" is not to be found in the claim of the person to be loved, but in the heart of the one who loves. If my heart is right with God, every human being is my neighbor. There is engrained in the depths of human nature a dislike of the general ruck of mankind, in spite of all our modern jargon about loving humanity. We have a disparaging way of talking about the common crowd; the common crowd is made up of innumerable editions of you and me. Ask the Holy Spirit to enable your mind to brood for one moment on the value of the "nobody" to Jesus. The people who make up the common crowd are nobodies to me, but it is astonishing to find that it is the nobodies that Jesus Christ came to save. The terms we use for men in the sense of their social position are nothing to Him. There is no room in Christianity as Jesus Christ taught it for philanthropic or social patronage. Jesus Christ never patronized anyone, He came right straight down to where men live in order that the supreme gift He came to give might be theirs—"The Spirit of the LORD is upon Me, because He has anointed Me to preach the gospel to the poor" (Luke 4:18). It is only by getting our minds into the state of the mind of Jesus that we can understand how it is possible to fulfill the royal law and love our neighbor as ourselves. We measure our generosity by the standards of men; in effect Jesus says, "Measure your love for men by God's love for them, and if you are My disciple, you will love your neighbor as I have loved you."

Holiness

Imitated Holiness

> . . . Leaving us an example, that you should follow His steps.
> (1 Peter 2:21)

For one child to imitate another child only results in a more or less clever affectation; a child imitating his parents assists the expression of inherent tendencies, naturally and simply, because he is obeying a nascent instinct. It is to this form of imitation that Peter alludes. When a saint imitates Jesus, he does it easily because he has the Spirit of Jesus in him. Pharisaic holiness, both ancient and modern, is a matter of imitation, seeking by means of prayer and religious exercises to establish, seriously and arduously, but unregeneratedly, a self-determined holiness. The only spiritually holy life is a God-determined life. "Be holy; for I am holy" (1 Peter 1:16, quoting Leviticus 11:44, el al.). If our best obedience, our most spotless moral walking, our most earnest prayers are offered to God in the very least measure as the ground of our acceptance by Him, it is a fatal denial of the Atonement.

Imputed Holiness

> . . . To whom God imputes righteousness apart from works.
> (Romans 4:6)

To *impute* means to "attribute vicariously"; it is a theological word. The revelation made by the apostle Paul, namely that God

imputes righteousness to us, is the great truth at the basis ᴄ
our Protestant theology; we are apt to forget this toda,
Righteousness means living and acting in accordance with right
and justice; that is, it must express itself in a man's bodily life.
"Little children, let no one deceive you. He who practices
righteousness is righteous" (1 John 3:7). Imputed righteousness
must never be made to mean that God puts the robe of His
righteousness over our moral wrong—like a snow drift over a
rubbish heap, that He pretends we are all right when we are not.
The revelation is that "Christ Jesus . . . became for us . . .
righteousness" (1 Corinthians 1:30); it is the distinct impartation
of the very life of Jesus on the ground of the Atonement, enabling
me to walk in the light as God is in the light, and as long as I
remain in the light God sees only the perfections of His Son. We
are "accepted in the Beloved" (Ephesians 1:6).

Imparted Holiness

> not having my own righteousness . . . but that which is
> through faith in Christ. (Philippians 3:9)

The only holiness is the holiness derived through faith, and
faith is the instrument the Holy Spirit uses to organize us into
Christ. But do not let us be vague here. Holiness, like sin, is a
disposition, not a series of acts. A man can act holy but he has
not a holy disposition. A saint has had imparted to him the
disposition of holiness, therefore holiness must be the
characteristic of the life here and now. Entire sanctification is the
end of the disposition of sin but only the beginning of the life of a
saint; then comes growth in holiness. The process of
sanctification begins at the moment of birth from above and is
consummated on the unconditional surrender of my right to
myself to Jesus Christ. The time that elapses between new birth
and entire sanctification depends entirely on the individual. Many
souls have had such a blessed vision of an entirely sanctified life

ntions or in times of rare communion with God that
they have the reality, and it is at this stage that that
y, "Deeper death to self" is apt to lead them astray.
s followed by a deep valley of humiliation, by a cross
fore the unspeakable reality is realized. If we have
reached the stage of entire sanctification and have presented our
bodies "a living sacrifice, holy, acceptable to God" (Romans 12:1),
what are we doing with our holy selves? Jesus Christ gives us the
key to the life of the saints: "And for their sakes I sanctify
Myself" (John 17:19). We are sanctified for one purpose only,
that we might sanctify our sanctification, that is, deliberately give
it to God.

Habitual Holiness

> Be transformed by the renewing of your mind. (Romans
> 12:2)

Practical holiness is the only holiness of any value in this
world and the only kind the Spirit of God will endorse. If we
consider what Professor James says in his scientific exposition of
habit, it will be a great rebuke to our lazy neglect in finding out
what we have to do to work out in actual life the holy disposition
given us through the Atonement.
1. In the acquisition of a new habit, or the leaving off of an old
one, we must launch ourselves with as strong and decided
initiative as possible.
2. Never suffer an exception to occur till the new habit is
securely rooted in your life.
3. Seize the very first possible opportunity to act on every
resolution you make and on every emotional prompting you may
experience in the direction of the habits you aspire to gain.
    Romans 12:2 is the apostle Paul's passionate entreaty that
we should rouse ourselves out of that stagnation that must end in
degeneration in which we are ensnared by thinking because it is

all of grace, there is no need for gumption. Grace, grit, glory is the graduation course. Professor James says "we must launch ourselves with as strong and decided initiative as possible": as saints have we not a strong and decided initiative? Born again of the Spirit, cleansed from all sin, sanctified to do the will of God? "Be transformed by the renewing of your mind," says Paul. It is because we have failed to realize that God requires intellectual vigor on the part of a saint that the devil gets his hold on the stagnant mental life of so many. To be transformed by the renewing of our minds means the courageous lifting of all our problems—individual, family, social and civic—into the spiritual domain and habitually working out a life of practical holiness there. It is not an easy task, but a gloriously difficult one, requiring the mightiest effort of our human nature, a task that lifts us into thinking God's thoughts after Him.

"That you may prove what is the good and acceptable and perfect will of God" (Romans 12:2). God's will is only clearly understood by the development of spiritual character; consequently, saints interpret the will of God differently at different times. It is not God's will that alters, but the saint's development in character. Only by intense, habitual holiness, by the continual renewing of our minds, and by the maintenance of an unworldly spirit can we be assured of God's will concerning us, "that good and acceptable and perfect will of God."

The Mature Christian

Therefore you shall be perfect, just as your Father in heaven
is perfect. (Matthew 5:48)

In Matthew 5:29–30; 48, our Lord refers to two things that
are full of vital instruction. In verses 29–30 He is referring to the
necessity of a maimed life: "If your right eye causes you to sin,
pluck it out and cast it from you"; in verse 48, He refers to the
life that is not maimed, but perfect. These two statements
embrace the whole of the spiritual life from beginning to end.

"Therefore you shall be perfect, just as your Father in
heaven is perfect." God is so almightily simple that it is
impossible to complicate Him, impossible to put evil into Him or
bring evil out of Him, impossible to alter His light and His love;
the nature of the faith born in me by the Holy Spirit will take
me back to the source and enable me to see what God is like,
and until I am all light and all love in Him, the things in me that
are not of that character will have to pass. In the beginning of
Christian experience the life is maimed because we are learning.
There is the right eye to be plucked out, the right hand to be cut
off, and we are apt to think that is all God means; it is not.
What God means is what Jesus said, "You shall be perfect, just
as your Father in heaven is perfect." When we discern that the
sword that is brought across the natural life is not for
destruction, but for discipline, we get His idea exactly. God
never destroys the work of His own hands; He removes what
would pervert it, that is all. Maturity is the stage where the
whole life has been brought under the control of God.

The Upward Look

Psalm 121 portrays the upward look: "I will lift up my eyes to the hills—from whence comes my help? My help comes from the LORD, who made heaven and earth" (verse 1). The upward look of a mature Christian is not to the mountains, but to the God who made the mountains. It is the maintained set of the highest powers of a man—not stargazing till he stumbles—but the upward gaze deliberately set toward God. He has got through the choppy waters of his elementary spiritual experience and now he is set on God. "I have set the LORD always before me" (Psalm 16:8)—but you have to fight for it.

The Forward Look

"Your eyes will see the King in His beauty; they will see the land that is very far off" (Isaiah 33:17). The forward look is the look that sees everything in God's perspective whereby His wonderful distance is put on the things that are near. Caleb had the perspective of God; the men who went up with him saw only the inhabitants of the land as giants and themselves as grasshoppers (see Numbers 13). Learn to take the long view and you will breathe the benediction of God among the squalid things that surround you. Some people never get ordinary or commonplace. They transfigure everything they touch because they have got the forward look that brings their confidence in God out into the actual details of life. The faith that does not react in the flesh is very immature. Paul was so identified with Jesus Christ that he had the audacity to say that what men saw in his life in the flesh was the very faith of the Son of God. Galatians 2:20 is the most audacious verse in the Bible! Paul is not referring to his own elementary faith in Jesus Christ as his Savior, but to the faith of the Son of God, and he says that that identical faith is now in him.

Fortitude in trial comes from having the long view of God. No matter how closely I am imprisoned by poverty or tribulation, I see the land that is very far off, and there is no drudgery on earth that is not turned divine by the very sight. Abraham did not always have the forward look; that is why he did a scurry down to Egypt when there was a famine in the Land of Promise. Why shouldn't I starve for the glory of God? As soon as I fix on God's "goods," I lose the long view. If I give up to God because I want the hundredfold more, I never see God.

The Backward Look

> Your ears shall hear a word behind you saying, "This is the way, walk in it," whenever you turn to the right hand or whenever you turn to the left. (Isaiah 30:21)

The surest test of maturity is the power to look back without blinking anything. When we look back we get either hopelessly despairing or hopelessly conceited. The difference between the natural backward look and the spiritual backward look is in what we forget. Forgetting in the natural domain is the outcome of vanity—the only things I intend to remember are those in which I figure as being a very fine person! Forgetting in the spiritual domain is the gift of God. The Spirit of God never allows us to forget what we have been, but He does make us forget what we have attained, which is quite unnatural. The surest sign that you are growing in mature appreciation of your salvation is that as you look back you never think now of the things you used to bank on. Think of the difference between your first realization of God's forgiveness and your realization of what it cost God to forgive you; the hilarity in the one case has been merged into holiness; you have become intensely devoted to God who forgave you.

Perfect Love

But whoever keeps His word, truly the love of God is perfected in him. (1 John 2:5)

If we love one another, God abides in us, and His love has been perfected in us. (1 John 4:12)

In Abandoned Indwelling

There is only one Being who loves perfectly, and that is God, yet the New Testament distinctly states that we are to love as God does; so the first step is obvious. If ever we are going to have perfect love in our hearts we must have the very nature of God in us. In Romans 5:5, the apostle Paul tells us how this is possible; he says: "the love of God has been poured out in our hearts by the Holy Spirit who was given to us." Paul is speaking not of the power to love God, but of the very love of God itself that has been poured out—a superabounding word. It means that the love of God takes possession of every crook and cranny of our natures. The practical question to ask therefore is, "Have I received the Holy Spirit? Has it ever come to an issue with me?" There is nothing on earth like the love of God when it breaks on the soul; it may break at a midnight or at dawn but always as a great surprise, and we begin to experience the uniting of the whole being with the nature of God. Everything in that moment becomes easy, no command of Jesus is difficult to obey. It is not our power to love God that enables us to obey, but the presence of the very love of God in our hearts that makes it so easy to obey Him that we don't even know we are obeying. As you recall to your mind the touchings of the love of God in your life they are always few—you will never find it impossible to do anything He asks.

When the love of God has been poured out in our hearts we have to exhibit it in the strain of life; when we are saved and sanctified we are apt to think that there is no strain, but Paul speaks of the "tribulation" that "produces perseverance" (verse 3). I mean by *strain* not effort, but the possibility of going wrong as well as of going right. There is always a risk, for this reason, that God values our obedience to Him. When God saves and sanctifies a man his personality is raised to its highest pitch of freedom, he is free now to sin if he wants to; before, he was not free, sin was impelling and urging him; when he is delivered from sin he is free not to sin or free to sin if he chooses. The doctrine of sinless perfection and consequent freedom from temptation runs on the line that because I am sanctified, I cannot now do wrong. If that is so, you cease to be human. If God put us in such a condition that we could not disobey, our obedience would be of no value to Him. But blessed be His name, when by His redemption the love of God is poured out in our hearts, He gives us something to do to manifest it. Just as human nature is put to the test in the actual circumstances of life, so the love of God in us is put to the test. "Keep yourselves in the love of God," says Jude 21; that is, keep your souls open not only to the fact that God loves you, but that He is in you, in you sufficiently to manifest His perfect love in every condition in which you can find yourselves as you rely upon Him. The curious thing is that we are apt, too apt, to restrain the love of God; we have to be careless of the expression and heed only the source. Let our Lord be allowed to give the Holy Spirit to a man, deliver him from sin, and put His own love within him, and that man will love Him personally, passionately, and devotedly. It is not an earning of or a working for, but a gift and a receiving.

In Abandoned Identification

Love suffers long and is kind. (1 Corinthians 13:4)
For the love of Christ compels us. (2 Corinthians 5:14)

The Holy Spirit pours out the love of God in our hearts and in 1 Corinthians 13 we see how that perfect love is to be expressed in actual life. "Love suffers long and is kind." Substitute "the Lord" for "love," and it comes home. Jesus is the love of God incarnate. The only exhibition of the love of God in human flesh is our Lord, and John says "as He is, so are we in this world" (1 John 4:17). God expects His love to be manifested in our redeemed lives. We make the mistake of imagining that service for others springs from love of others; the fundamental fact is that supreme love for our Lord alone gives us the motive power of service to any extent for others: "ourselves your bondservants for Jesus' sake" (2 Corinthians 4:5). That means I have to identify myself with God's interests in other people, and God is interested in some extraordinary people—namely, in you and in me, and He is just as interested in the person you dislike as He is in you. I don't know what your natural heart was like before God saved you, but I know what mine was like. I was misunderstood and misrepresented; everybody else was wrong and I was right. Then when God came and gave me a spring-cleaning, dealt with my sin, and filled me with the Holy Spirit, I began to find an extraordinary alteration in myself. I still think the great marvel of the experience of salvation is not the alteration others see in you, but the alteration you find in yourself. When you come across certain people and things and remember what you used to be like in connection with them and realize what you are now by the grace of God, you are filled with astonishment and joy; where there used to be a well of resentment and bitterness there is now a well of sweetness.

God grant we may not only experience the indwelling of the

love of God in our hearts, but go on to a hearty abandon to that love so that God can pour it out through us for His redemptive purposes for the world. He broke the life of His own Son to redeem us, and now He wants to use our lives as a sacrament to nourish others.

Sacramental Christianity

The word *sacramental* must be understood to mean the real presence of Christ being conveyed through the actual elements of the speech and natural life of a Christian: "Therefore whoever confesses Me before men" (Matthew 10:32), that is, confesses with every part of him that "Jesus Christ has come in the flesh"—has come, not only historically, but in the Christian's own flesh.

Sacramental Service

> But God forbid that I should boast except in the cross of our Lord Jesus Christ, by whom the world has been crucified to me, and I to the world. (Galatians 6:14)

By the Cross of Christ I am saved from sin, by the Cross of Christ I am sanctified, but I never am a sacramental disciple until I deliberately lay myself on the altar of the Cross and give myself over emphatically and entirely to be actually what I am potentially in the sight of God, namely, a member of the body of Christ. When I swing clear of myself and my own consciousness and give myself over to Jesus Christ, He can use me as a sacrament to nourish other lives. Most of us are on the borders of consciousness, consciously serving, consciously devoted to God; it is all immature, it is not the life yet. Maturity is the life of a child—a child is never consciously childlike—so abandoned to God that the thought of being made broken bread and poured-out wine no longer unseals the fountain of tears. When you are conscious of being used as broken bread and poured-out wine you are interested in your own martyrdom; it is consciously costing you something. When you are laid on the altar of the Cross all consciousness of self is gone, all consciousness of what you are doing for God or of what God is doing through you is gone. It is no longer possible to talk about "my experience of sanctification"; you are brought to the place where you understand what is meant by our Lord's words, "You shall be witnesses to Me" (Acts 1:8). Wherever a saint goes, everything he does becomes a sacrament in God's hands, unconsciously to him. You never find a saint being consciously used by God; God uses some casual thing you never thought about, which is the surest evidence that you have got beyond the stage of conscious sanctification; you are beyond all consciousness because God is taking you up into His consciousness; you are His, and life becomes the natural, simple life of a child. To be everlastingly on the lookout to do some work for God means I want to evade sacramental service—"I want to do what I want to do." Maintain the attitude of a child toward God and God will do what He likes with you. If God puts you on the shelf, it is in order to season you. If He is pleased to put you in limited circumstances so that you cannot go out into the highways of service, then enter into sacramental service. Once you enter that service, you can enter no other.

Sacramental Fellowship

> Unless a grain of wheat falls into the ground and dies, it remains alone; but if it dies, it produces much grain. (John 12:24)

If you are wondering whether you are going on with God, examine yourself in the light of these words. The more spiritually real I become, the less am I of any account; I become more and more of the nature of a grain of wheat falling into the earth and dying in order that it may bring forth fruit. "He must increase, but I must decrease" (John 3:30). I only decrease as He increases, and He only increases in me as I nourish His life by that which decreases me. Am I willing to feed the life of the Son of God in me? If so, then He increases in me. There is no pathos in John's words, but delight: "Would to God I could decrease more quickly!" If a man attracts by his personality, then his appeal must come along the line of the particular work he wishes to do; but stand identified with the personality of your Lord, like John the Baptist, and the appeal is for His work to be done. The danger is to glory in men—"What a wonderful personality!" If when people get blessed they sentimentally moon around me, I am to blame because in my heart I lay the flattering unction to myself that it is because of my way of putting things; they begin to idealize the one who should be made broken bread and poured-out wine for them. Beware of stealing souls, for whom Christ died, for your own affectionate wealth.

Sacramental Responsibility

> I now rejoice in my sufferings for you, and fill up in my flesh what is lacking in the afflictions of Christ, for the sake of His body, which is the church. (Colossians 1:24)

By "sacramental responsibility" understand the solemn determination to keep myself notably my Lord's and to treat as a subtle temptation of the devil the call to take on any responsibility that conflicts with my determined identification with the Lord's interests. God's one great interest in men is that they are redeemed; am I identifying myself with that interest? Notice where God puts His disapproval on human experiences: it is when we begin to adhere to our conception of what sanctification is and forget that sanctification itself has to be sanctified. When we see Jesus we will be ashamed of our deliberately conscious experience of sanctification; that is the thing that hinders Him because instead of other people seeing Jesus in me, they see me and not Jesus. We have to be sacramental elements in His hands not only in word, but in actual life. After sanctification it is difficult to state what your aim in life is because God has taken you up into His purposes. The design for God's service is that He can use the saint as His hands or His feet. Jesus taught that spiritually we should grow as the lilies, bringing out the life that God blesses.

His Certain Knowledge

... for He knew what was in man. (John 2:25)

Our Lord seemed to go so easily and calmly amongst all kinds of men. When He met a man who could sink to the level of Judas, He never turned cynical, never lost heart or got discouraged; when He met a loyal loving heart like John's, He was not unduly elated, He never overpraised him. When we meet extra goodness we feel amazingly hopeful about everybody, and when we meet extra badness we feel exactly the opposite, but Jesus "knew what was in man." He knew exactly what human beings were like and what they needed, and He saw in them something no one else ever saw—hope for the most degraded. Jesus had a tremendous hopefulness about man.

How Jesus Thought about Man

Everything Jesus Christ thought about man is summed up in the parable of the two sons (see Luke 15), namely: that man had a noble origin, that he sinned willfully, and that he has the power to return if he will. Do we accept Jesus Christ's view, or do we make excuses for ourselves? "Oh well, I am trying my best, and I am getting a little better every day"—no one ever did! Numbers of us get a little worse every day. "I didn't mean to go wrong." It was not only our great forerunner who sinned willfully, there is a willful element in every one of us; we sin knowing it is sin. Socrates' notion was that if you tell a man what is right, he will do it, but he neglected the big factor that a man's innermost instinct is not God. There is a potential hero in every man—and a potential skunk.

Jesus Christ's thought about man is that he is lost and that He is the only One who can find him. "For the Son of Man has come to seek and to save that which was lost" (Luke 19:10). Salvation means that if a man will turn—and every man has the power to turn, if it is only a look toward the Cross, he has the power for that—if a man will but turn, he will find that Jesus is able to deliver him not only from the snare of the wrong disposition within him, but from the power of evil and wrong outside him. The words of Jesus witness to His knowledge that man has the power to turn: "Come to Me" (Matthew 11:28). "The one who comes to Me I will by no means cast out" (John 6:37). As soon as a man turns, God finds him. The Cross of Christ spells hope for the most despairing sinner on the face of the earth. "The Son of Man has power on earth to forgive sins" (Matthew 9:6).

How Jesus Treated Men

Jesus Christ treated men from the standpoint of His knowledge of them—He is the supreme Master of the human heart. Recall what He said, "For from within, out of the heart of men, proceed evil thoughts" (Mark 7:21); consequently He was never surprised, never in a panic. When He met the rich young ruler, an upright, splendid young man, we read that "Jesus looking at him, loved him" (Mark 10:21), but He knew that at the back of all his morality was a disposition that could sin willfully against God. "If you want to be perfect . . ." (Matthew 19:21), then come the conditions. Again, when Jesus met Nicodemus, a godly man, a ruler of the synagogue, He told him he must be made all over again before he could enter the kingdom of God (see John 3:1–21). Or think how Jesus treated Peter. Peter loved Jesus, he declared that he was ready to lay down his life for Him, yet he denied Him thrice. But Jesus never lost heart over him. He had told him beforehand: "I have prayed for you, that your faith should not fail; and when you have returned to Me, strengthen your brethren" (Luke 22:32). Sin never frightened Jesus; the devil never frightened Him. Face Jesus Christ with all the power of the devil: He was manifested that He might destroy the works of the devil. Are you being tripped up by the subtle power of the devil? Remember, Jesus Christ has power not only to release you, but to make you more than conqueror over all the devil's onslaughts.

"For He knew what was in man"—consequently He never trusted any man, whether it was John or Peter or Thomas; He knew what was in them. They did not. How wonderfully the apostle Paul learned this lesson! Read his epistles—"Don't glory in men, glory only in Jesus Christ and in His work in you." The Holy Spirit applies Jesus Christ's knowledge to me until I know that "in me [that is, in my flesh] nothing good dwells" (Romans 7:18), consequently I am never dismayed at what I discover in myself but learn to trust only what the grace of God does in me.

How does Jesus Christ treat me? Let me receive the Holy Spirit and I will very soon know. He will treat me as He treats every man—mercilessly with regard to sin. We say, "O Lord, leave a little bit of pride, a little bit of self-realization." God can never save human pride. Jesus Christ has no mercy whatever when it comes to conviction of sin. He has an amazing concern for the sinner but no pity for sin.

How Jesus Thought about Himself

"For in that He Himself has suffered, being tempted, He is able to aid those who are tempted. . . . [He] was in all points tempted as we are, yet without sin" (Hebrews 2:18; 4:15). These verses reveal that it was in His temptation our Lord entered into identification with our need. He took upon Him our human nature, our flesh and blood, and the Spirit drove Him into the wilderness to be tempted by the subtle power of the antagonist of God. Having suffered, being tempted He knows how terrific are the onslaughts of the devil against human nature unaided; He has been there, therefore He can be touched with the feeling of our infirmities. God Almighty was never tempted in all points as we are; Jesus Christ was. God Almighty knows all that Jesus Christ knows, but, if I may say it reverently, God in Christ knows more because God in Christ suffered being tempted, and therefore He is able to aid those who are tempted.

Those of you who have been saved by God's grace, have you accepted Jesus' thought about men and are you learning to treat them as He did? Or has your soul been rushed into a moral panic as you faced a difficult case? If so, you have never begun to think in Christ's school. If you are rightly related to God there is no excuse for indulging in panic; the Holy Spirit will safeguard you from alarm at immorality and put you in the place where you can "fill up . . . what is lacking in the afflictions of Christ" (Colossians 1:24). If you suffer from panic, you hinder the Holy Spirit working through you. It is easy to be shocked at immorality, but how much education in the school of Christ, how much reliance on the Holy Spirit, does it take to bring us to the place where we are shocked at pride against God? That sensitivity is lacking today.

"And because lawlessness will abound, the love of many will grow cold" (Matthew 24:12). The portrait of many of us was sketched in these words of Jesus. Think of the worst man you know—not the worst man you can think of, because that is vague—have you any hope for him? Does the Holy Spirit begin to convey to your mind the wonder of that man being presented perfect in Christ Jesus? That is the test as to whether you have been learning to think about men as Jesus thought of them. The Holy Spirit brings us into sympathy with the work Jesus has done on behalf of men in that He is "able to save to the uttermost those who come to God through Him" (Hebrews 7:25).

How the Apostle Paul Returns Thanks

Indeed I have all and abound. I am full, having received from Epaphroditus the things sent from you, a sweet-smelling aroma, an acceptable sacrifice, well pleasing to God. (Philippians 4:18)

The apostle Paul refused to take money help from any of the churches he founded and over which he watched so carefully, and his reasons for this are expounded in 1 Corinthians 9 (see also a significant reference in Acts 20:34), the one exception being the church at Philippi. Paul's imprisonment had revived their affectionate interest, and he writes to thank them for a further gift through Epaphroditus, as "even in Thessalonica you sent aid once and again for my necessity" (Philippians 4:16). The epistle is a letter of gratitude for these gifts, and along with his thanks Paul combines solicitations and teaching and deals with some of the grandest, most fundamental truths, for example, in chapter 2.

The letter is addressed to "all the saints in Christ Jesus who are in Philippi" from "Paul and Timothy, bondservants of Jesus Christ" (1:1). This is a wonderfully courteous touch; Paul does not call himself here an apostle of Jesus Christ, but by a name that embraces Timothy because Timothy was with him when the church was founded—"bondservants of Jesus Christ."

Chapter 1

> But I want you to know, brethren, that the things which
> happened to me have actually turned out for the furtherance
> of the gospel. (1:12)

The fortune of misfortune! That is Paul's way of looking at
his captivity. He does not want them to be depressed on his
account or to imagine that God's purpose has been hindered; he
says it has not been hindered, but furthered. The very things that
looked so disastrous have turned out to be the most opportune,
so that on this account his heart bounds with joy, and the note of
rejoicing comes out through the whole letter.

> Some indeed preach Christ even from envy and strife, and
> some also from goodwill. (1:15)

Paul was severity itself in dealing with those in Galatia who
preached the gospel from the wrong motive (see Galatians 1:7–8;
2:4–5, 8; 5:4–5); here, he deals with the matter more gently. What
is the reason for the difference? In the first case false brethren had
insinuated themselves into the church with the set purpose of
unsettling the believers and bringing them into bondage; in this
case the motive, he says, was "to add affliction to my chains"
(1:16). Whenever harm is being done to the flock of God it must
be tracked out and dealt with rigorously; personal injury is
another matter. "Whoever slaps you on your right cheek, turn the
other to him also" (Matthew 5:39), said our Lord, and Paul
exhibits that spirit when he says, "What then? Only that in every
way, whether in pretense or in truth, Christ is preached; and in
this I rejoice, yes, and will rejoice" (Philippians 1:18).

This brings us up against a big problem, a problem our Lord
refers to in Matthew 7:21–23. Because God honors His word no
matter how preached or by whom, we naturally infer that if His

word is blessed and souls are saved, demons are cast out, mighty works are done, surely the preacher must be a servant of God. It does not follow by any means. An instrument of God and a servant of God ought to be identical, but our Lord's words and Paul's are instances where they are not. It does not impair the inspiration of the gospel to have it preached by a bad man, but the influence of the preacher, worthy or unworthy, apart altogether from his preaching, has a tremendous effect. If I know a man to be a bad man, the sinister influence of his personality neutralizes altogether the effect of God's message through him to me, but let me be quite sure that my intuition springs from my relationship to God and not from human suspicion.

Chapter 2

> Fulfill my joy by being like-minded, having the same love, being of one accord, of one mind. (2:2)

In 2:1–4 Paul is arguing, "If you are rightly related to God in Christ, the life of the Son of God in you makes you identical with Him, so that the same comfort of love, the same fellowship of the Spirit, the same mercies that marked Him, mark you." How we water down the amazing revelation of the New Testament that we are made one with Christ! I live; yet not I, but Christ lives in me (see Galatians 2:20).

> Let this mind be in you which was also in Christ Jesus. (2:5)

We are not given a fully formed, reasoning Christian mind when we are born again. We are given the Spirit of Jesus but not His mind; we have to form that. The mind Paul urges the Philippian Christians to form is not the mind of almighty God, but the mind of Christ Jesus, "who, being in the form of God, did not consider it robbery to be equal with God" (verses 5–6). This was the central citadel of the Temptation—"You are the Son of

God, assert your prerogative; You will bring the world to Your feet if You will remember who You are and use Your power" (see Matthew 4:1–11). The answer Jesus made was, "I do not seek My own will"; in essence, "Although I am the Son of God, I am here in this order of things for one purpose only, to do the will of My Father" (see John 5:30). When we are sanctified the same temptation comes to us—"You are a child of God, identified with Jesus, presume on it, think it something to be grasped, to be proud of." We are saved and sanctified for one purpose, that God's will might be done in us as it was in our Lord.

> Work out your own salvation with fear and trembling; for it is God who works in you both to will and to do for His good pleasure. (Philippians 2:12–13)

These verses combine all we understand by the great efficacious work of the grace of God in salvation and sanctification. "You are saved," says Paul, "now work it out: be consistent in character with what God has worked in." The only estimate of consistent Christian character is the life of Jesus being made manifest in our mortal flesh. People talk a lot about their experience of sanctification and too often there is nothing in it. It doesn't work out in the bodily life or in the mind, it is simply a doctrine; with Paul it was the mainspring of his life. "For it is God who works in you . . . to will." It is nonsense to talk about a man's free will; a man's will is only fundamentally free in God. That is, he is only free when the law of God and the Spirit of God are actively working in his will by his own choice.

> . . . that you may become blameless and harmless, children of God without fault in the midst of a crooked and perverse generation among whom you shine as lights in the world. (2:15).

That means on this earth, not in heaven. We have to shine

as lights in the squalid places of earth; we can't shine in heaven—our light would be put out in two seconds. "That you may become blameless"—if ever we are to be blameless, undeserving of censure in the sight of God who sees down to the motive of our motives, it must be by the supernatural power of God. The meaning of the Cross is just that—I not only can have the marvelous work of God's grace done in my heart, but can have the proof of it in my life. The "Higher Christian Life" phraseology is apt to be nothing in the world but the expression of a futile and sorrowful struggle, adoring God for what we are in His divine anticipation but never can be in actuality. It is only when I realize that God's anticipations for me are presented as participations through the power of the Holy Spirit that I become that peculiarly humble person, a disciple of the Lord Jesus.

> Yes, and if I am being poured out as a drink offering on the sacrifice and service of your faith, I am glad and rejoice with you all. (2:17)

Paul's conception of the altar of sacrifice is spending and being spent for the sake of the elementary children of God. He has no other end and aim than that—to be broken bread and poured-out wine in the hands of God so that others might be nourished and fed (cf. Colossians 1:24). The great Savior and His great apostle go hand-in-hand: the Son of God sacrificed Himself to redeem men; Paul, His bondservant, sacrificed himself that men might come to know they are redeemed, that they have been bought with a price and are not their own; it was no false note when Paul said, Christ lives in me.

Chapter 3

> . . . concerning the law, a Pharisee. (3:5)

Saul of Tarsus did easily what all other Pharisees did, but

his conscience would not allow him to be a hypocrite easily. His ardent nature tried to make his inner life come up to the standard of the law, and the tragedy of his failure is portrayed in Romans 7. No one was ever so introspective, so painfully conscious of weakness and inability to keep the law as Paul, so when he says, "Christ is the end of the law for righteousness" (Romans 10:4), he is making an intensely practical statement. He is stating the fact that Jesus Christ has planted in him as a sheer gift of God's grace the life that enables him now to fulfill all the law of God—"not having my own righteousness, which is from the law, but that which is through faith in Christ, the righteousness which is from God by faith" (Philippians 3:9). *Imputed* means "imparted" with Paul.

> If anyone else thinks he may have confidence in the flesh, I more so. (3:4)

In 3:4–6, Paul catalogs the things that used to be "gains" to him, the things that were a recommendation to him in the eyes of the world (cf. Galatians 1:13–14), but, he says, "I fling them all overboard as refuse, that I may win Christ." The whole of Paul's life has been redetermined by regeneration, and he estimates now from an entirely different standard. The things from which we have to loose ourselves are the good things of the old creation as well as the bad, for example, our natural virtues because our natural virtues can never come anywhere near what Jesus Christ wants.

> . . . that I may know Him and the power of His resurrection, and the fellowship of His sufferings. (3:10)

Paul talks more about suffering than any of the apostles, but any suffering that is less than fellowship with *His* sufferings he treats very lightly: "our light affliction" (2 Corinthians 4:17); "sufferings . . . are not worthy to be compared with the glory"

(Romans 8:18). Jesus suffered according to the will of God, and to be made a partaker of His sufferings destroys every element of self-pity, of self-interest, of self-anything.

> Not that I . . . am already perfected. (3:12)
> Therefore let us, as many as are mature [perfect KJV]. (3:15)

Nothing but willful perversion would make anyone misunderstand these two *perfects.* In 3:12, Paul is speaking of the perfection of consummation not attainable in this life; in 3:15 he speaks of a perfection of fitness demanded now. Remember, though you are perfectly adjusted to God, you have attained to nothing yet. The idea is that of a marathon runner practicing and practicing until he is perfectly fit; when he is perfectly fit he hasn't begun the race, he is only perfectly fit to begin. By regeneration we are put into perfect relationship to God; then, we have the same human nature working along the same lines but with a different mainspring. "Not that I . . . am already perfected": that is the perfection of consummation; "I haven't got there yet," says Paul, "but I press on, that I may lay hold of that for which Christ Jesus has also laid hold of me" (3:12). Paul was absolutely Christ-centered; he had lost all interest in himself in an absorbing, passionate interest in Christ. Very few saints get where he got, and we are to blame for not getting there. We thank God for saving and sanctifying us and continually revert to these experiences. Paul reverted to one thing only: "When it pleased God . . . to reveal His Son in me" (Galatians 1:15–16), then he never bothered any more about himself. We try to efface ourselves by an effort; Paul did not efface himself by an effort. His interest in himself simply died right out when he became identified with the death of Jesus.

> For many walk, of whom I have told you often, and now tell you even weeping, that they are the enemies of the cross of

Christ." (3:18)

Why did Paul say "enemies of the cross of Christ," not "enemies of Christ"? The test all through is trueness to the Cross. What the enemies of the Cross so strenuously oppose is identification on the part of the believer with what the death of Christ on the Cross represents, namely, death to sin in every shape and form. Look at the tremendous words Paul uses; they express the agony of his heart over those who are the enemies of that moral identification. Their god is themselves—what develops me, not that which takes me right out of the road and gives the Son of God a chance to manifest Himself in me. What was it God condemned in the Cross? Self-realization. Have I come to a moral agreement with God about that? To say that what God condemned in the Cross was social sins is not true; what God condemns in the Cross is sin, which is away further down than any moral quirks.

Chapter 4

> Therefore, my beloved and longed-for brethren, my joy and crown, so stand fast in the Lord, beloved. (4:1)

Notice Paul's earnest solicitation over those who have been saved through his ministry; he carried every convert on his heart to the end of his life or of theirs.

> Be anxious for nothing. (4:6)

The enemy of saintliness is anxiousness over the wrong thing. The culture of the Christian life is to learn to be carefully careless over everything except our relationship to God. It is not sin that keeps us from going on spiritually, but the cares of the world, the lusts of other things that crowd out any consideration of God. We reverse the teaching of Jesus; we don't seek first the kingdom of God. We seek every other thing first, and the result accords with what Jesus said, the word He puts in is choked and becomes unfruitful.

> Finally, brethren, whatever things are true, . . . meditate on these things. (4:8)

Glean your thinking—one of the hardest things to do. For instance, it is essentially difficult to think along the lines laid down in 1 Corinthians 13:4–5: "Love . . . thinks no evil"; apart from God we do think of evil, we reason from that standpoint. The majority of us are not spiritual thinkers, but when we begin to think on the basis of our relationship to God through the redemption we find it a most revolutionary thing. We are not saved by thinking, we form our *nous,* a responsible intelligence, by thinking, and as soon as we face the application of the redemption to the details of our lives, we find it means everything has to be readjusted bit by bit.

Problemata Mundi

Have you considered My servant Job, that there is none like him on the earth, a blameless and upright man, one who fears God and shuns evil? (Job 1:8)

The book of Job mirrors for all time the problem of things as they have been, as they are, and as they will be until they are altered by the manifestation of a new heaven and a new earth. When things go well a man does not want God, but when things get difficult and suffering begins to touch him, he finds the problem of the world inside his own skin. The slander of men is against God when disasters occur. If you have never felt inclined to call God cruel and hard, it is a question whether you have ever faced any problems at all. Job's utterances are those of a man who suffers without any inkling as to why he suffers, yet he discerns intuitively that what is happening to him is not in God's order although it is in His permissive will. All through, Job stands for two things: that God is just and that he himself is relatively innocent. Remember, Job was never told the preface to his own story; he did not know that he had been chosen to be the battleground between God and Satan. Satan's contention was that no man loved God for His own sake—"Does Job fear God for nothing?" (1:9) "Job only loves You because You bless him. Let me curse his blessings and I will prove it to You." Satan's primary concern is to sneer against God; he is after disconcerting God, putting God in a corner, so to speak, where He will have to take action along Satan's proposed lines.

There are circumstances in life that make us know that Satan's sneer is pretty near the mark. I love God as long as He blesses me, saves my soul, and puts me right for heaven; but supposing He should see fit to let the worst things happen to me, would I say, "Go on, do it," and love Him still? The point is that God's honor is at stake in a man who suffers as did this blameless and upright man. Part of the problem was that in the bargain Satan made with God, Satan implied that God must keep out of sight, and God did. He never once showed Himself to Job. The presentation of the controversy between God and Satan is such that Satan has everything on his side and God nothing on His, so much so that God dare not say a word to Job till he had proved himself worthy. Job cannot answer one of the charges the friends bring against him. He tears their arguments to shreds in the fervor of his pain, yet he clings to it: "I will believe God in spite of everything that seems to be contradicting His character."

The apostle James (see 5:11) talks about the patience of Job—Job patient! He was patient but only to God. There is nothing logical about Job, his statements are wild and chaotic, but underneath there is an implicit understanding of God's character. He is sure of God even though He seems to be doing everything to ruin him, and he draws steadily nearer God as his friends withdraw themselves from him heaping their anathemas upon him. They slander Job while standing up for God, but in the end God says, "You have not spoken of Me what is right, as My servant Job has" (42:7). The citadel of true religion is personal relationship to God, let come what will.

Where does your mind rest regarding suffering? The Bible makes little of physical suffering. The modern mind looks on suffering and pain as an unmitigated curse; the Bible puts something akin to purifying in connection with suffering, for instance "he who has suffered in the flesh has ceased from sin" (1 Peter 4:1). The thing that moves us is the pathos arising from physical suffering; the anguish of a soul trying to find God we put down to lunacy. The only way traditional belief can be transformed into personal possession is by suffering. Look at what you say you believe; not an atom of it is yours except the bit you have proved by suffering and in no other way. Never run away with the idea that Satan is skeptical of all virtue, he knows God too well and human nature too well to have such a shallow skepticism; he is skeptical only of virtue that has not been tried. Faith untried is simply a promise and a possibility, which we may cause to fail; tried faith is the pure gold. Faith must be tried, otherwise it is of no worth to God. Think of the dignity it gives to a man's life to know that God has put His honor in his keeping. Our lives mean more than we can tell: they mean that we are fulfilling some purpose of God about which we know nothing any more than Job did. God's government of the world is not for material prosperity, but for moral ends, for the production of moral characters, in the sense of holy characters. Time is nothing to God.

"The LORD gave Job twice as much as he had before. . . . Now the LORD blessed the latter days of Job more than his beginning" (42:10, 12). The charge is made that, because God gave Job back his material prosperity, therefore the whole argument of the book falls to the ground, but the blessing of God on Job was nothing more than an outward manifestation accompanying the certainty he now possessed, namely, that he loves God and that God loves him. It is the overflowing favor of God poured out on a loved son who has come through the ordeal and won his way straight through to God.

A Fatal Error of Indignant Integrity

He was angry and would not go in. (Luke 15:28)

We get the idea that wrong views of God and of goodness arise from a life that is wrong; the Bible shows that wrong views of God and of goodness may arise out of a life that is right. The parable of the two sons is an example of this. The younger brother was a wastrel; the elder brother was a man of integrity, there was not a spot on his character—"I never transgressed your commandment at any time" (Luke 15:29). Everything that led him to take up the position he did was perfectly justifiable; it was the protest of an upright man, but he made the fatal error of misinterpreting his father's ways and refusing to enter into a love that was too big for this earth. Many good, upright people misinterpret God's ways because they do not take into account, first of all, the matter of personal relationship to God. They say because we are the creatures of God, we are the sons and daughters of God; Jesus Christ taught with profound insistence that we are sons and daughters of God only by an inner disposition, the disposition of love, that works implicitly. The Bible states that "love is of God" (see 1 John 4:7–16). The difficulty arises out of our individuality, which is hard and tight, segregated from others; personality is never isolated, it always merges and is characterized by an implicit understanding of things. The attitude of the elder brother is individual entirely, he is merged into nothing of the nature of love; consequently he misunderstands his father and demands that his ways ought to be more clearly justifiable to human reason. God's ways never are because the basis of things fundamentally is not reasonable; if it were, God would be cruel to allow what He does. Our reason is simply an instrument, the way we explain things; it is not the basis of things. The problems of life are only explainable by means of a right relationship to God. If we ask for a reasonable explanation of God's ways in providence, such as are stated in the book of Job, or in the puzzles of nature referred to by Paul in Romans 8:19–23, we will end in misinterpreting God, but when we receive the disposition Jesus Christ came to give us, we find our problems are explained implicitly. There is no such thing as sin to commonsense reasoning, therefore no meaning in the Cross because that view rules out what the Bible bases everything on, namely, the hiatus between God and man produced by sin and the Cross where sin is dealt with. When commonsense reasoning comes to the Cross it is embarrassed; it looks at the death of Jesus as the death of a martyr, One who lived beyond His dispensation. According to the New Testament, the Cross is the Cross of God, not of a man. The problems of providence, the puzzles of nature, the paradoxes of Christianity do not bother everybody; they are the problems of men who are good and upright but distinctly individual, and their individuality causes them to misinterpret God's ways and to repudiate Christianity.

"As soon as this son of yours came, who has devoured your livelihood with harlots, you killed the fatted calf for him" (Luke 15:30). The elder brother is right, not wrong, according to all reasonable human standards, when he says of the prodigal, "Such a character ought not to be allowed in the home, he ought to be excluded." A bad man would have said, "Oh, well, it doesn't matter, he has made mistakes, we all do." Embarrassment always arises in the domain of ethics when we make the basis of Christianity adherence to principles instead of personal relationship to God. What is called Christianity, our charity and benevolence, is not Christianity as the New Testament teaches it; it is simply adherence to certain principles. Jesus tells us to "give to him who asks you" (Matthew 5:42)—not because he deserves it or because he needs it, but "because I tell you to" (see Matthew 5:43–48). Ask yourself, "Do I deserve all I have got?" The teaching of Jesus revolutionizes our modern conception of charity.

A false idea of God's honor ends in misinterpreting His ways. It is the orthodox type of Christian who, by sticking to a crude idea of God's character, presents the teaching that says, "God loves you when you are good but not when you are bad." God loves us whether we are good or bad. That is the marvel of His love. "I have not come to call the righteous, but sinners, to repentance" (Luke 5:32)—whether there are any righteous is open to question. "The righteous have no need of Me; I came for the sinful, the ungodly, the weak." If I am not sinful and ungodly and weak, I don't need Him at all.

The presentation Jesus gives of the father is that he makes no conditions when the prodigal returns, neither does he bring home to him any remembrance of the far country—the elder brother does that. It is the revelation of the unfathomable, unalterable, amazing love of God. We would feel much happier in our backslidden condition if only we knew it had altered God toward us, but we know that as soon as we do come back we will find Him the same, and this is one of the things that keeps us from coming back. If God would only be angry and demand an apology, it would be a gratification to our pride. When we have done wrong we like to be lashed for it. God never lashes. Jesus does not represent the father as saying, "You have been so wicked that I cannot take you back as my son, I will make you a servant," but as saying:

> Bring out the best robe and put it on him, and put a ring on his hand and sandals on his feet. And bring the fatted calf here and kill it, and let us eat and be merry; for this my son was dead and is alive again; he was lost and is found. (Luke 15:22–24)

Divine Paradox

There is probably no more prominent feature in Bible revelation than that of paradox. In Revelation 5:5–6, the apostle John records that in his vision he was told "the Lion of the tribe of Judah . . . has prevailed to open the scroll" and, he says, "behold, in the midst of the throne . . . stood a Lamb"! We find a paradox of a similar nature in Isaiah 63:1. The prophet has been looking for some great, conquering army of the Lord, and instead he sees a lonely Figure, "traveling in the greatness of His strength." If you take all the manifestations of God in the Old Testament you find them a mass of contradictions: now God is pictured as a man, now as a woman, now as a lonely hero, now as a suffering servant, and until we come to the revelation in the New Testament these conflicting characteristics but add confusion to our conception of God. But as soon as we see Jesus Christ, we find all the apparent contradictions blended in one unique person.

Drummond, in his *Natural Law in the Spiritual World*, surely makes a fundamental blunder by that very statement, and surely the contention in Butler's *Analogy* is right—that as there is a law in the natural world so there is also a law in the spiritual world but that they are not the same laws; the one is the complement of the other. Unless this is borne in mind by the student of Scripture and he learns to rely on the Holy Spirit to interpret the spiritual law as he relies on his own spirit to interpret the natural law, he will not only end in confusion, but will be in danger of disparaging the spiritual law in the Bible universe in favor of the natural law in the commonsense universe.

And I saw in the right hand of Him who sat on the throne a
scroll . . . sealed with seven seals. (Revelation 5:1)

I am considering the book in one aspect only, namely, as
containing a knowledge of the future, an understanding of the
providence of God in the present, together with a grasp of the
past. The deepest clamor of a man's nature once he is awake is to
know the whence and whither of life: Whence came I? Why am
I here? Where am I going? In all ages men have tried to pry into
the secrets of the future; astrologers, necromancers, spiritualists,
or whatever name you may call them by, have all tried to open the
book, but without success, because it is a sealed book. "I wept
much," says John, "because no one was found worthy to open and
read the scroll, or to look at it" (5:4).

Because of the sealed character of the book men become
indifferent and cease to be exercised over the whence and whither
of human destiny; they take no interest in Bible revelation and are
amused at our earnest solicitation on their behalf—"It is all about
something we cannot know, and there is no one who can tell us."
Others say, "There is nothing to know"; not, "We cannot know,"
or "There is nothing to know; a man lives his life, then dies, and
that is all there is." The psalmist refers to such men when he says,
"The fool has said in his heart, 'There is no God' " (Psalm 14:1).
There are others whose sensitive spirits give them an implicit
sense that there is more than this life; there are hidden deeps in
their hearts that human life and its friendships can never satisfy.
The scenes of earth, its sunsets and sunrises, its "huge and
thoughtful nights," all awaken an elemental sadness that makes
them wonder why they were born, and they feel keenly because
the book is sealed and there is no one able to open it.

But would to God all men knew that there is Someone who
is worthy to open the book!

But one of the elders said to me, "Do not weep. Behold, the
Lion of the tribe of Judah, the Root of David, has prevailed

to open the scroll and to loose its seven seals. (Revelation 5:5)

Who is this Worthy One? If one may say it with reverence, realizing the limitation of language, God Himself had to be proved worthy to open the book. In the person of Jesus Christ God became man, He trod this earth with naked feet,

> *and wrought*
> *with human hands the creed of creeds*
> *In loveliness and perfect deeds.*

By His holy life, by His moral integrity and supreme spiritual greatness, Jesus Christ proved that He was worthy to open the book. The book can be opened by only one hand, the pierced hand of the Worthy One, our Savior Jesus Christ.

The childish idea that because God is great He can do anything, good or bad, right or wrong, and we must say nothing is erroneous. The meaning of moral worth is that certain things are impossible to it: "it is impossible for God to lie" (Hebrews 6:18); it is impossible for Jesus Christ to contradict His own holiness or to become other than He is. The profound truth for us is that Jesus Christ is the Worthy One not because He was God incarnate, but because He was God incarnate on the human plane. "Coming in the likeness of men" (Philippians 2:7), He accepted our limitations and lived on this earth a life of perfect holiness. Napoleon said of Jesus Christ that He had succeeded in making of every human soul an appendage of His own—why? because He had the genius of holiness. There have been great military geniuses, intellectual giants, geniuses of statesmen, but these only exercize influence over a limited number of men; Jesus Christ exercizes unlimited sway over all men because He is the altogether Worthy One.

> And I looked, and behold, in the midst of the throne . . .
> stood a Lamb as though it had been slain. (Revelation 5:6)

Jesus Christ is the supreme sacrifice for the sin of the world; He is "the Lamb of God, who takes away the sin of the world!" (John 1:29). How the death of Jesus looms all through the Bible! It is through His death that we are made partakers of His life and can have gifted to us pure hearts, which He says is the condition for seeing God.

"Having . . . seven eyes" (Revelation 5:6). The Lamb is not only the supreme sacrifice for man's sin, He is the searcher of hearts, searching to the inmost recesses of mind and motive. It is not a curious searching, not an uncanny searching, but the deep, wholesome searching the Holy Spirit gives in order to convict men of their sin and need of a savior; then when they come to the Cross, and through it accept deliverance from sin, Jesus Christ becomes the Sovereign of their lives, they love Him personally and passionately, beyond all other loves of earth.

> Then He came and took the scroll out of the right hand of
> Him who sat on the throne. (5:7)

Jesus Christ, and He alone, is able to satisfy the craving of the human heart to know the whence and whither of life. He enables men to understand that they have come into this life from a deep purpose in the heart of God, that the one thing they are here for is to get readjusted to God and to become His lovers. And where are we going? We are going to where the Book of Life is opened and we enter into an effulgence of glory we can only conceive of now at rare moments.

In the days of His flesh Jesus Christ exhibited this divine paradox of the Lion and the Lamb. He was the Lion in majesty, rebuking the winds and the demons; He was the Lamb in meekness, "who, when He was reviled, did not revile in return" (1Peter 2:23). He was the Lion in power, raising the dead; He was the Lamb in patience, who was "led as a lamb to the slaughter, and as a sheep before its shearers is silent, so He opened not His mouth" (Isaiah 53:7). He was the Lion in authority: "You have heard that it was said. . . . But I say to you . . ." (see Matthew 5:21–48); He was the Lamb in gentleness: " 'Let the little children come to Me,' . . . and He took them up in His arms, laid His hands on them, and blessed them" (Mark 10:14–16).

In our personal lives Jesus Christ proves Himself to be all this—He is the Lamb to expiate our sins, to lift us out of condemnation and plant within us His own heredity of holiness; He is the Lion to rule over us so that we gladly say, "The government of this life shall be upon His shoulders." And what is true in individual life is to be true also in the universe at large. The time is coming when the Lion of the tribe of Judah shall reign and when "the kingdoms of this world" shall become "the kingdoms of our Lord and of His Christ" (Revelation 11:15).

One remaining paradox: In Revelation 6:16, "the wrath of the Lamb" is mentioned. We know what the wrath of a lion is like—but the wrath of the Lamb—it is beyond our conception. All one can say about it is that the wrath of God is the terrible obverse side of the love of God.

Memory of Sin in the Saint

He counted me faithful, putting me into the ministry, although I was formerly a blasphemer, a persecutor, and an insolent man. (1 Timothy 1:12–13)

And such were some of you. (1 Corinthians 6:11)

No aspect of Christian life and service is in more need of revision than our attitude to the memory of sin in the saint. When the apostle Paul said, "forgetting those things which are behind" (Philippians 3:13), he was talking not about sin, but about his spiritual attainment. Paul never forgot what he had been; it comes out repeatedly in the Epistles: "For I am the least of the apostles, who am not worthy to be called an apostle" (1 Corinthians 15:9); "To me, who am less than the least of all the saints, this grace was given" (Ephesians 3:8); "sinners, of whom I am chief" (1 Timothy 1:15). And these are the utterances of a ripe, glorious servant of God.

If one wants a touchstone for the depth of true spiritual Christianity, one will surely find it in this matter of the memory of sin. There are those who exhibit a Pharisaic holiness; they thank God with an arrogant offensiveness that they are not as other men are; they have forgotten the horrible pit and miry clay from where they were taken and their feet set upon a rock through the might of the Atonement. Perhaps the reason they condemn others who have fallen and been restored is the old human failing of making a virtue out of necessity. Their lives have been shielded, the providence of God has never allowed them to be enmeshed in the subtle snares other men have encountered whose fall has plunged them into an agony of remorse. May the conviction of God come with swift and stern rebuke upon anyone who is remembering the past of others, and deliberately choosing to forget their restoration through God's grace. When a servant of God meets these sins in others, let him be reverent with what he does not understand and leave God to deal with them.

Certain forms of sin shock us far more than they shock God. The sin that shocks God, the sin that broke His heart on Calvary, is not the sin that shocks us. The sin that shocks God is the thing that is highly esteemed among us—self-realization, pride, my right to myself. We have no right to have the attitude to any man or woman as if he or she had sunk to a lower level than those of us who have never been tempted on the line they have. The conventions of society and of our social relationships make it necessary for us to take this attitude, but we have to remember that in the sight of God there are no social conventions and that external sins are not a bit worse in His sight than pride that hates the rule of the Holy Spirit though the life is morally clean. May God have mercy on any one of us who forgets this and allows spiritual pride or superiority and a sense of his own unsulliedness to put a barrier between him and those whom God has lifted from depths of sin he cannot understand.

Holiness is the only sign that a man is repentant in the New Testament sense, and a holy man is not one who has his eyes set on his own whiteness, but one who is personally and passionately devoted to the Lord who saved him—one whom the Holy Spirit takes care shall never forget that God has made him what he is by sheer sovereign grace. Accept as the tender touch of God, not as a snare of the devil, every memory of sin the Holy Spirit brings home to you keeping you in the place where you remember what you once were and what you now are by His grace.

"This is a faithful saying and worthy of all acceptance, that Christ Jesus came into the world to save sinners; of whom I am chief" (1 Timothy 1:15)—sinners, of whom I am chief. What a marvelous humility it betokens for a man to say that and mean it! In the early days of the sterner form of Calvinism, a man's belief about God and about his own destiny frequently produced a wistful, self-effacing humility, but the humility Paul manifests was produced in him by the remembrance that Jesus, whom he had scorned and despised, whose followers he had persecuted, whose church he had harried, had not only forgiven him, but had made him His chief apostle: "To me, who am less than the least of all the saints, this grace was given, that I should preach among the Gentiles the unsearchable riches of Christ" (Ephesians 3:3).

"However for this reason I obtained mercy, that in me first Jesus Christ might show all longsuffering, as a pattern to those who are going to believe on Him for everlasting life" (1 Timothy 1:16). Here is the the attitude of the servant of God—"since God has done this for me, I can despair of no one on the face of the earth." Show such a servant of God the backslider, the sinner steeped in the iniquity of our cities, and there will spring up in his heart an amazing well of compassion and love for that one, because he has himself experienced the grace of God that goes to the uttermost depths of sin and lifts to the highest heights of salvation.

But where sin abounded, grace did abound more exceedingly.

Celebration or Surrender?

We begin our Christian lives by believing what we are told to believe; then we have to go on to so assimilate our beliefs that they work out in a way that redounds to the glory of God. The danger is in multiplying the acceptance of beliefs we do not make our own. Every now and again we find ourselves lost in wonder at the marvel of the redemption; it is a wholesome initial stage but if it is made the final stage it is perilous. The difficulty of believing in the redemption in the sense of assimilating it is that it demands renunciation. I have to give up my right to myself in complete surrender to my Lord before what I celebrate becomes a reality. There is always the danger of celebrating what Jesus Christ has done and forgetting the need on our part of moral surrender to Him; if we evade the surrender we become the more intense in celebrating what He has done.

The Snare of Emotional Rapture

> Then Peter answered and said to Jesus, "Rabbi, it is good for us to be here. (Mark 9:5)

Be quick to notice how God brings you rapidly from emotional rapture into contact with the sordid, commonplace activities of life. There are times in the providence of God when He leads us apart by ourselves, when Jesus reveals Himself to us and we see Him transfigured. The place apart by ourselves may be a prayer meeting, a service, a talk with a friend, a sunrise, or a sunset when we are stirred to the depths and see what we are unable to utter. The snare is to imagine that that is all God means; He means much more. "And a cloud came and overshadowed them; and a voice came out of the cloud, saying, "This is my beloved Son. Hear Him'." (Mark 9:7)—not, "This is My beloved Son; now spend halcyon days with Him on the mount." Beware of celestial sensuality. No matter what your experience, you may be trapped by sensuality anytime. Sensuality is not sin; it is the way the body works in connection with circumstances whereby I begin to satisfy myself. Mary Magdalene was in danger of making this blunder but Jesus said, "Do not cling to Me" (John 20:17)—"Don't try and hold Me by your senses, but go and do what I say." Always thrust out into the actual because it is there you exhibit whether your emotional rapture has seduced you, made you unfit for activities.

[handwritten margin note: calm, tranquil → halcyon]

After a time of rapt contemplation when your mind has been absorbing the truth of God, watch the kind of people God will bring round you: not people dressed in the cast-off nimbus of some saint, but ordinary, commonplace people just like you. We imagine that God must engineer special circumstances for us, peculiar sufferings; He never does, because that would feed our pride; He engineers things that, from the standpoint of human pride, are a humiliation.

"Suddenly, when they had looked around they saw no one anymore, but only Jesus with themselves" (Mark 9:8). Instead of "no cross, no crown" spiritually (William Penn) it is no crown, no cross. We are crowned by the moment of rapture, but that is not the end; it is the beginning of being brought down into the demon-possessed valley to bear the cross for Him there. With a sudden rush we find no Moses, no Elijah, no transfiguration glory, and we fear as we enter the cloud till we come to the place where there is "no one anymore, but only Jesus." As men and women we have to live in this world, in its misery and sinfulness, and we must do the same if we are disciples. Of all people we should be able to go down into the demon-possessed valley because once we have seen Jesus transfigured it is impossible to lose heart or to be discouraged.

Celebration or Surrender   121

The Sincerity of Experimental Realization

> Yet indeed I also count all things loss for the excellence of
> the knowledge of Christ Jesus my Lord. (Philippians 3:8)

Paul goes on to state that he not only estimated the cost, he experienced it: "for whom I have suffered the loss of all things . . . that I may gain Christ and be found in Him, not having my own righteousness" (verses 8–9). Imagine anyone who has seen Jesus Christ transfigured saying he is sorry to find himself mean and ignoble! The more I whine about being a miserable sinner the more I am hurting the Holy Spirit. It simply means I don't agree with God's judgment of me; I think, after all, that I am rather desirable—God thought me so undesirable that He sent His Son to save me. To discover I am what God says I am ought to make me glad; if I am glad over anything I discover in myself, I am very shortsighted. The only point of rest is in the Lord Himself.

> *Since mine eyes have looked on Jesus,*
> *I've lost sight of all beside . . .*
> *So enhanced my spirit's vision*
> *Gazing on the Crucified.*

THE SERVANT
AS HIS LORD

Yet it was well, and Thou hast said in season,
    "As is the Master shall the servant be":
Let me not slide into the treason,
    Seeking an honor which they gave not Thee.

      . . .

Yea, thro' life, death, thro' sorrow and thro' sinning
    He shall suffice me, for He hath sufficed:
Christ is the end, for Christ was the beginning,
    Christ the beginning, for the end is Christ.

                         F. W. H. Myers

The Fighting Chance

Romans 8:35–39

The Mental Field

> Who shall separate us from the love of Christ? Shall
> tribulation, or distress? (Romans 8:35)

During the French Revolution little boys who could not
much more than walk carried a banner around with the words,
"Tremble, tyrants, we are growing" printed on it. That is the
aspect I want us to look at. We are not meant to be carried to
heaven "on flow'ry beds of ease" (Watts). We are given the
fighting chance, and it is a glorious fight. Jesus Christ came to
fit men to fight. He came to make the lame, the halt, the
paralyzed, the all but sin-damned into terrors to the prince of
this world.

If there is one thing an unsaved man is incapable of doing, it
is fighting against the awful powers of sin. He can fight in the
physical realm because he has the spirit of lust; but Paul warns
that "We do not wrestle against flesh and blood, but against . . .
the spiritual hosts of wickedness in the heavenly places"
(Ephesians 6:12). No man is a match for that warfare unless he is
saved by God's grace. "Therefore take up the whole armor of
God" (verse 13). Fancy telling a man to put on the armor of God
while he has a traitor on the inside! A man has to put on the
armor of God to fight in when he has had the lustful disposition
taken out of him. For what purpose? that he may fight all that

comes against him and come off more than conqueror. Have you ever seen Jesus Christ take a man who has been paralyzed by sin, paralyzed by a wrong past, by a present that makes him say, "I shall never be different"—have you ever seen Jesus Christ take that man and turn him into a fighter, one who can turn to flight armies of aliens? (see Hebrews 11:34). That is what Jesus Christ can do by His marvelous salvation; He can put into a man, whose energy has been sapped by sin and wrong until he is all but in hell, a life so strong and full that Satan has to flee whenever he meets him. Is there a man here who would not give his right arm, nay, his very life, if God would fit him to fight and make him more than conqueror over sin and Satan and circumstances? Thank God, He can do it! Oh, let me repeat it. I do not care how defaced you may be morally, how weak and backslidden, I do know that Jesus Christ can make you more than conqueror as you draw on His resurrection life.

"The fighting chance" exactly describes the way we are made. Take our bodies: we are kept healthy by our capacity to fight, and the stronger the forces within the better is our health. Health simply means a perfect balance between the body and the outer world. The same is true mentally. I continually come across people with rusty "thinkers"; they think about their business but about nothing else, and the forces within have become desperately weak; consequently when tribulation comes their minds are confused, and the result is that errors come into the life. If the forces within are strong and healthy they give us warning and enable us to crush in a vice on the threshold of the mind everything that ought not to come there. God can impart to a man the power to select what his mind thinks, the power to think only what is right and pure and true.

If it is a fight in the physical and mental realm, it is also a fight in the spiritual realm, only tremendously intensified because when we receive the new life from God, Satan instantly brings all his power to crush it out. But thank God, no matter how the enemy presses God can make us more than conquerors because the very life of Jesus is imparted to us and we are able to face the devil and to face sin as Jesus did.

Predicted

> In the world you will have tribulation; but be of good cheer,
> I have overcome the world. (John 16:33; cf. 17:14–16).

Jesus Christ foretold tribulation; He conveyed His message with a clarion voice to the saints in all ages: "In the world you will have tribulation"; the apostle Paul continually warns us that we have no right to settle on our lees: "For in fact, we told you before when we were with you that we would suffer tribulation, just as it happened, and you know" (1 Thessalonians 3:4). Tribulation means being thronged by severe affliction and trouble; that is what the saints are to expect in this dispensation and not be astonished when it comes. God allows tribulation and anguish to come right to the threshold of our lives in order to prove to us that His life in us is more than a match for all that is against us. When we see the awfulness of evil in this world we imagine there is no room for anything but the devil and wrong, but this is not so. God restrains the powers of evil. How does He do it? Through the lives of the saints who are pushing the battle everywhere their feet are placed. The devil tackles on the right hand and on the left, but they are more than conquerors; they not only go through the tribulation, but are "exceeding joyful" in it.

Portrayed

> O Jerusalem, Jerusalem, the one who kills the prophets and stones those who are sent to her! How often I wanted to gather your children together, as a hen gathers her chicks under her wings, but you were not willing!" (Matthew 23:37; see Romans 9:1–3)

Have you ever noticed the examples the New Testament gives of those who go through tribulation? our Lord Himself and the apostle Paul. The writer to the Hebrews says, "Consider Him" (Hebrews 12:3). Have you ever considered Jesus Christ's distress over Jerusalem? Do we know anything about that kind of tribulation? There is a difference between the distress that comes to our human minds and the distress of the Holy Spirit through us. Jesus warned that "because lawlessness will abound, the love of many shall grow cold" (Matthew 24:12). Why? because people are not rooted in the right place. No matter how iniquity may abound or how crushing may be the afflictions that throng around, Jesus Christ can make us more than conquerors while at the same time we taste the anguish of the Holy Spirit.

A great danger besets Christians, and Satan is at the back of it, namely, the danger that makes men and women think that they are God's favorites. No one can monopolize God; it is easy to say that, yet we seem to think we can. God has no favorites, but when we let Him have His right of way through us He begins to unveil something more of His purposes in our lives. Has God unfolded to you His purpose in your family? in your business? in Battersea? wherever you are? Or is tribulation making you wilt? making you swoon for sympathy? making you stagnate? It is an easy business to want to get away from tribulation, but fighting makes us strong, gloriously strong.

Are you saying, "I wonder if I am ever going to get out of these circumstances? if things are ever going to alter for me?" Let God alter you, let Him put within you the life of His Son and, backed by Almighty God, you will not only get the fighting chance, but you will glory in tribulation—the tramp of the conqueror about you. God grant we may let our hearts talk to our minds and let our minds follow on to know; we can only know by means of this tribulation experience.

When you have to go and see some "big" person, remember to take a deep breath and you will be surprised to find how courageous you feel. Apply that spiritually: when there is tribulation and distress thronging round you, take time and draw in a tremendous draught of the grace of God, and you will find it is a delight to meet it because He makes us more than conquerors in the midst of it all.

The Moral Field

Who shall separate us from the love of Christ? Shall . . . persecution? (Romans 8:35)

Morality is not something with which we are gifted, we make morality; it is another word for character. "Unless your righteousness [i.e., your morality] exceeds the righteousness of the scribes and Pharisees," said Jesus, "you will by no means enter the kingdom of heaven" (Matthew 5:20). Morality is not only correct conduct on the outside, but correct thinking within where only God can see. No matter how a man may have been tampered with by Satan, God can remake him so that in every moral battlefield he can come off more than conqueror. Thank God He does give us the fighting chance! In certain moods we are inclined to criticize God for not making the world like a foolproof machine whereby it would be impossible to go wrong. If God had made men and women like that we would have been of no worth to Him. Jesus Christ, by His almighty redemption, makes us of the stuff that can stand the strain.

One afternoon I was watching the birds on the lake in Battersea Park and I got a splendid illustration of persecution. There were all kinds of birds—ducks and seagulls and swans, and some birds not native to our shores. Children were feeding them, and one white duck got hold of a crust. Immediately the other ducks tried to grab it from her, but she swam through her own crowd, easily outwitting them. Then the foreign birds swooped down on her, a new style of enemy, but I never saw rabbit or boy chase and turn with such dexterity as that duck, and over and over again the seagulls struck the water instead of the duck. Then along came the cygnets and tried to pull the duck back by main force and take the crust from her, but the more they tackled, the more dexterous she got, until at last she cleared them all and got complete victory. That is exactly the meaning of persecution— systematic vexation.

Place

> But he who received the seed on stony places, this is he who hears the word and immediately receives it with joy; yet he has no root in himself, but endures only for a while. For when tribulation or persecution arises because of the word, immediately he stumbles. (Matthew 13:20–21)

The first place where you meet persecution is after conversion. I am not using the word *conversion* in the sense of regeneration, but in the sense of being in the condition to receive something from God (see Acts 26:18). As soon as you turn in the direction of God and receive a word from Him, you will find systematic vexation begin on that particular word—"for when tribulation or persecution arises because of the word, immediately he stumbles." The proof that you have the root of the matter in you is that you easily prevail against persecution. How many of us have turned aside at the very outset, at conversionpoint, when we first begin to testify, because of persecution? Jesus Christ told us to expect it. I think we are losing sight of the real meaning of testimony; it is not for the sake of others, but for our own sake. It makes us know we have no one to rely on but God.

Persecution is not only met at the threshold, it increases as we go on in the Christian life. A man may get through persecution from his own crowd, but when it comes to persecution from principalities and powers, that is a domain he knows nothing about. When we are saved and sanctified God does not shield us from any requirement of a son or daughter of His; He lifts His hand off, as it were, and says to the devil, "Do your worst." "You are of God, little children, and have overcome them, because He who is in you is greater than he who is in the world" (1 John 4:4); we find to our delight that we are made more than conquerors. We talk about people being loved into blessing, but no one is loved into blessing unless he is first lured by that love to a tremendous surgical operation. There must be a radical alteration within before the new life is there that will overcome all that comes against it. Persecution is the thing that tests our Christianity, and it always comes in our own setting; the crowd outside never bothers us. To have brickbats and rotten eggs flung at you is not persecution; it simply makes you feel good and does you no harm at all. But when your own crowd cut you dead and systematically vex you, then says Jesus, "count it all joy." Leap for joy "when men hate you, and when they exclude you, and revile you, and cast out your name as evil, for the Son of Man's sake" (Luke 6:22–23)—not for the sake of some crotchety notion of your own.

Profit

> Blessed are you when they revile and persecute you, and say all kinds of evil against you falsely for My sake. Rejoice, and be exceedingly glad, for great is your reward in heaven. (Matthew 5:11–12; see 2 Corinthians 12:10)

Jesus Christ not only warned that persecution would come, He went further and said that it was profitable to go through persecution. "Blessed are you, when they . . . persecute you." The way the world treats me is the exhibition of my inner disposition. "Whoever therefore wants to be a friend of the world makes himself enemy of God" (James 4:4). The line where the world ends and Christianity begins alters in every generation. What was worldliness in Paul's day is not worldliness in our day; the line is altering all the time. Today the world has taken on so many things out of the church and the church has taken on so many things out of the world that it is difficult to know where you are. As soon as you let the disposition God gives you manifest itself, you are going to be a speckled bird. "My heritage is to Me like a speckled vulture," says Jeremiah (12:9). No matter how sweet and winsome you may be, you will come across something that positively detests you. "If the world hates you, you know that it hated Me before it hated you" (John 15:18). Do we know anything about it?

Is some discouraged soul saying, "If only God would give me different circumstances?" No one understands your circumstances but God, and He has given you the fighting chance to prove you can be more than conqueror in all these things. Let God lift you out of the broken place, out of the bedraggled place. Let Him put within you the Holy Spirit so that you can face the music of life and become more than conqueror in every place where you have been defeated. Carlyle said of Tennyson that he was always carrying about with him a lump of chaos and turning it into cosmos. That is another way of putting this truth, that we each make our own character. God gives us a new disposition, the disposition of His Son; then we have to work out what He has worked in, and the way we react in the circumstances God engineers for us produces character.

Have you ever noticed how God permits the natural virtues to break down? People whose lives have been moral and upright get astounded when these virtues begin to crumble. They have been trying to build up a character on these virtues, and it cannot be done. Natural virtues are not a promise of what we are going to be, but a remnant of what we once were. No natural virtue can come anywhere near the standard Jesus Christ demands. We have to receive the Holy Spirit and let Him bring us to the place where we are so identified with the death of Jesus that it is "no longer I who live, but Christ lives in me" (Galatians 2:20), and then go on to build up a character on the basis of Jesus Christ's disposition. The Christian life is drawn, from first to last and all in between, from the resurrection life of the Lord Jesus.

The Material Field

> Who shall separate us from the love of Christ? Shall . . .
> nakedness, or peril, or sword?" (Romans 8:35)

The material field, means things that come to a man's life from the outside—famine, nakedness, peril, sword. The apostle Paul seems to be never tired of comparing the Christian life to a fight, a fight against tremendous odds but always a winning fight. In these verses Paul brings before our contemplation every conceivable battlefield; every maneuver and strategy of the enemy is embraced, no phase of his tactics is left out, and in it all Paul says we are "more than conquerors through Him who loved us" (verse 37). We cannot be more than conquerors if there is nothing to fight! Our Lord Himself and the Spirit of God in the Epistles make it very clear that everything that is not of God will try its best to kill His life out of us, yet instead of doing that it makes us all the stronger. The love of God in Christ Jesus is such that He can take the most unfit man—unfit to survive, unfit to fight, unfit to face moral issues—and make him not only fit to survive and to fight, but fit to face the biggest moral issues and the strongest power of Satan and come off more than conqueror. The love of God in Christ Jesus through the mighty Atonement is such that it can do this for the feeblest, the most sinful man, if he will hand himself over to God.

The Book Martyrs

> Most assuredly, I say to you, when you were younger, you girded yourself and walked where you wished: but when you are old, you will stretch out your hands, and another will gird you, and carry you where you do not wish." (John 21:18; cf. John 16:2; Luke 10:19).

A martyr is one who is put to death for adherence to principles. Martyrdom is not peculiar to the Christian religion. Men and women who suffer death for adhering to principles are found in every religion under heaven and outside any religion; but the particular type of martyrdom we are referring to is that of those men and women who go to death because of obedience to the principles of the life of Jesus in them.

In 1 Corinthians 4:9, Paul mentions a strange training for the apostles. He says that "God has displayed us, the apostles, last [i.e., as the last item in the day's play in the theatre] as men condemned to death; for we have been made a spectacle to the world"; the writer to the Hebrews, reminding us of the witnesses of old, says the same thing: they were "destitute, afflicted, tormented" (11:37). We are apt to say that we are not called to martyrdom today, but I think we shall begin to find that we are, and to a crueler martyrdom than that of the early days, which was intense and fierce and then over.

Shall nakedness? Nakedness means to be destitute of clothing and shelter, destitute of all sustenance for life. God said to Satan concerning Job—"Behold, all that he has is in your power" (Job 2:12). That permission has never been withdrawn, and every now and again Satan gets permission from God to play havoc with all our material possessions. "For one's life does not consist in the abundance of the things he possesses" (Luke 12:15). If our lives are in our material possessions, and nakedness, peril, and sword tackle and destroy them, where is our faith? But if we bank on the love of God in Jesus Christ, He will make us more than conquerors in all these things. God grant we may put Him first. When Mary of Bethany broke the alabaster box of ointment on the feet of Jesus, the disciples were indignant and said, "Why this waste? For this fragrant oil might have been sold for much and given to the poor" (Matthew 26:8). Have you ever noticed how strangely Jesus answered them? "For you have the poor with you always, and whenever you wish you may do them good; but Me you do not have always" (Mark 14:7; cf. Matthew 26:11). Did Jesus mean that He had no care for the poor? that He did not understand what an awful, stinging, grinding thing it is to be poverty-stricken and destitute? No one on earth felt these things more keenly than Jesus did, but He was pointing out that, as His disciples, the great note for our lives is not sympathy with the poor, not an understanding of the needs of men, but an understanding of His point of view.

> Blessed are you when men hate you, and when they exclude you, and revile you, and cast out your name as evil, for the Son of man's sake. (Luke 6:22; cf. 1 Peter 4:4)

"All who desire to live godly in Christ Jesus will suffer persecution" (2 Timothy 3:12), says Paul, and our Lord says the same thing. Men will make you destitute of their society, they will cut you dead, and when they do speak of you, they will speak evil. No man knew this better than the apostle Paul, and what did he do? He despised being despised! Persecution is systematic vexation; it does not leave you alone, it is something that throngs you. But to be boycotted means to be left alone, destitute of the comrades you used to have—"they think it strange that you do not run with them in the same flood of dissipation, speaking evil of you" (1 Peter 4:4). But they don't know that you carry a wonderful kingdom within, a kingdom full of light and peace and joy, no matter how destitute and alone you may be on the outside. That is the wonderful work of the Lord in a man's soul. "Rejoice in that day, and leap for joy!" (Luke 6:23).

One of the things I remember during the Welsh Revival was the unspeakable presence of God. It was unlike anything I had ever felt before. You could feel the presence of God in the very atmosphere and tell the districts where it was and where it was not, and I remember coming to the conclusion that if a martyr felt the marvel of that presence he would not feel the pain. Another thing that struck me was that while many were getting right with God, others were content with the enthusiasm of the presence of God and bringing forth no "fruits worthy of repentance." (Luke 3:8). When shall we understand that God's method is repentance first and then the reviving life of God? If revival does not bring forth fruits worthy of repentance, it will end in riot and ultimately in ruin.

> As it is written: "For Yoursake we are killed all day long;
> we are accounted as sheep for the slaughter." (Romans
> 8:36)

Anesthesia means insensibility to pain, and there is such a thing as spiritual anesthesia: God put you to sleep while the thing hurts. Some Christians do not seem to know that they are going through things, they are so wonderfully upheld by the life and power of God within; when you begin to sympathize with them, they look at you in amazement, "Why, what have I been through?" They had never realized that the battle was on. The danger is to get taken up with external tribulations and trials and when we come to the end of the day to say, "Thank God, I have just got through!" Where is "the unsearchable riches of Christ" (Ephesians 3:8) about that? The grace of God will make us marvelously impervious to all the onslaughts of tribulation and persecution and destitution because we are seated in heavenly places in Christ Jesus and cannot be awakened up to self-pity. God sends His rough weather and His smooth weather, but we pay no attention to either because we are taken up only with the one central thing—the love of God in Christ Jesus.

Where are you placed in your circumstances? Is it tribulation and anguish that are perplexing you? Is it nervous trouble that is overcoming you, the nameless dread that comes from nerves that are all on fire and jangled? I firmly believe there is no type of mental or nervous disease over which Jesus Christ cannot make us more than conquerors as we draw on His resurrection life. Is your battlefield the moral one? persecution—systematic vexation—in your home because you have got right with God? persistent ridicule from those you work with because of your obedience to Jesus Christ? Jesus Christ can make you more than conqueror there. Remember, morality is produced by fight, not by dreaming, not by shutting our eyes to facts, but by being made right with God; then we can make our morality exactly after the stamp of Jesus Christ.

The Natural Maneuvers

> For I am persuaded that neither death nor life . . . shall be able to separate us from the love of God which is in Christ Jesus our Lord. (Romans 8:38-39)

Paul has cataloged the things over which we are more than conquerors—tribulation, anguish, persecution, famine, nakedness, peril, sword; now he seems to strike another note, a note of defiance: "For I am persuaded that neither death nor life . . . shall be able to separate us from the love of God which is in Christ Jesus our Lord."

> He conjures; he marshals before him; he names over in all their greatest horror every conceivable trouble which afflicts the soul of man; he calls them up and he passes them in review before him, and he bids them do their worst, and sets them all at defiance . . . Life is an infinitely worse thing than death, more terrible, more appalling.
>
> Dr. David Smith

The Great Dread—Death

Death is a great dread. It is easy to say that God is love until death has snatched away your dearest friend, then I defy you to say that God is love unless God's grace has done a work in your soul. Death means extinction of life as we understand it; our dead are gone and have left an aching void behind them. They do not talk to us, we do not feel their touch, and when the bereaved heart cries out, nothing comes back but the hollow echo of its own cry. The heart is raw; no pious chatter, no scientific cant can touch it. It is the physical calamity of death plus the thing behind it that no man can grasp that makes death so terrible. We have so taken for granted the comfort that Jesus Christ brings in the hour of death that we forget the awful condition of men apart from that revelation. Do strip your mind and imagination of the idea that we have comfort about the departed apart from the Bible; we have not. Every attempt to comfort a bereaved soul apart from the revelation Jesus Christ brings is a vain speculation. We know nothing about the mystery of death apart from what Jesus Christ tells us, but blessed be the name of God, what He tells us makes us more than conquerors so that we can shout the victory through the darkest valley of the shadow that ever a human being can go through.

The Bible reveals that death is inevitable: "and thus death spread to all men" (Romans 5:12). "It is appointed for men to die once" (Hebrews 9:27). Repeat that over to yourself. It is appointed to every one of us that we are going to cease to be as we are now, and the place that knows us now shall know us no more. We may shirk it, we may ignore it, we may be so full of robust health and spirits that the thought of death never enters—but it is inevitable.

Another thing: the Bible says that a certain class of man is totally indifferent to death, "for there are no pangs in their death" (Psalm 73:4). Over and over again the Bible points out that the wicked man, the Esau type of man, who is perfectly satisfied with life as it is has not the slightest concern about death—because he is so brave and strong? no, because he is incapable of realizing what death means. The powers that press from the natural world have one tendency, and one only, to deaden all communication with God.

One other thing: the Bible says there are those who are intimidated by death, "that through death He might destroy him who had the power of death, that is, the devil, and release those who through fear of death were all their lifetime subject to bondage" (Hebrews 2:14–15). The thought of death is never away from them; it terrorizes their days, it alarms their nights. Now read very reverently Hebrews 5:7: "who . . . when He had offered up prayers and supplications, with vehement cries and tears to Him who was able to save Him from death." Who is that? the Lord Jesus Christ. We cannot begin to fathom this passage; after years of meditation on it we come only to the threshold of realizing what Gethsemane represents. Jesus Christ can deliver from the dread of death: "through death He might destroy him who had the power of death, that is, the devil." Death has no terror for the man who is rightly related to God through Jesus Christ. "How blest the righteous when he dies!" Were there any terrors in the passing of the founder of the League of Prayer? It was a marvelous and glorious translation. "O death, where is your sting? O Hades where is your victory?" (1 Corinthians 15:55; cf. Hosea 13:14).—absolutely nullified, destroyed by the majestic might of the Atonement.

The Greatest Danger—Life

Life is a far greater danger than death. I want to say something, crudely, but very definitely: the Bible nowhere says that men are damned; the Bible says that men are damnable. There is always the possibility of damnation in any life, always the possibility of disobedience, but, thank God, there is also always the possibility of being made more than conqueror. The possibilities of life are awful. Think—are you absolutely certain that you are not going to topple headlong over a moral precipice before you are three years older? Look back on your life and ask yourself how it was you escaped when you were set on the wrong course—the tiniest turn and you would have been a moral ruin. Disease cut off with a tremendous fell swoop your companions—why did it not cut you off? The men with you in your youth who were so brilliant—where are they now? out in the gutter some of them, all but damned while they live. Why are you not there? Why am I not there? Oh, it does us good, although it frightens us, to look at the possibilities of life. May God help us to face the issues.

Unless a man's peace and prosperity are based on a right relationship to God, it may end in a sudden and terrible awakening. We never know whether the next moment is going to bring us face-to-face with green pastures or a hurricane. The Bible reveals that here is a ruling principle at work in this world that hates God, and when we take sides against that principle there is the very devil to face. That is the apostle Paul's argument here. When we are born again into the heavenly kingdom, then come tribulation and anguish, then come persecution and famine, then come nakedness, peril, and sword; then comes life and then comes death—mocking us with paradoxes and puzzles we cannot explain. The possibilities and perils of life are enormous. It is only when some such considerations get hold of men who are bound up in a show of things that they begin to see the need for Jesus Christ's redemption.

The Greater Deliverance

I have been drawing a very dark picture you say. I have not. It is not within the power of human tongue or archangel's tongue to state what an awful fact death is and what a still more awful fact life is. But thank God, there is the greatest deliverance conceivable from all that life may bring and from all that death may bring. Jesus Christ has destroyed the dominion of death, and He can make us fit to face every problem of life, more than conquerors all along the line.

Let God have His way; He will turn the drama of your life into a doxology, and you will understand why the psalmist breaks out with the words, "Oh, that men would give thanks to the LORD for His goodness, and for His wonderful works to the children of men!" (Psalm 107:8, 15, 21, 31). Jesus Christ can make the weakest man into a divine dreadnought fearing nothing. He can plant within him the life that was in Himself, the life time cannot touch. "Most assuredly, I say to you, he who believes in Me has everlasting life" (John 6:47), that is, the life Jesus had, so that a man can face all the powers of hell with a conqueror's tread. Heroics? no; heroism. Heroics sound all very well on a stage, or on paper, but heroism works in flesh and blood, and

Jesus Christ makes us flesh-and-blood dreadnoughts. Not all the power of the enemy can fuss or turn aside the soul that is related to God through the Atonement.

The Supernatural Maneuvers

> For I am persuaded that neither . . . angels nor principalities nor powers . . . shall be able to separate us from the love of God which is in Christ Jesus our Lord. (Romans 8:38–39)

By the help of God's Spirit I want, for one moment, to lift the veil from the unseen world as the Bible reveals it that we may understand what a marvelous salvation we have, a salvation that keeps us not only from dangers we see and know, not only from sin and all we understand as the works of the devil, but a salvation that keeps us from dangers we know nothing about. Oh, there are tremendous possibilities around us! The Bible reveals that the unseen world has rulers and majesties and tremendous beings with whom man can get into communication and by whom he can be possessed, but God pronounces His curse on the man or woman who dares to communicate with them.

Messengers of the Unseen Universe

neither angels. The Bible has a great deal to say about angels: there are angelic hosts (see Matthew 26:53, Hebrews 1:7, 14) and angelic helpers (see Psalm 91:11–12; Matthew 18:10). When we were taught as children that angels watch around our beds it was not a fairy story we were told, but a revelation fact. The angels are there to guard us, and they watch and guard every blood-bought soul. And there is an angelic hell; there is no other place for fallen angels (Matthew 25:41; Jude 6; Revelation 20:10). It is never stated that God has provided a place for men who will not come to Him; it is implied with solemn warning that the only place they can go to is that "prepared for the devil and his angels" (Matthew 25:41).

The good angels are a host and the bad angels are a host. Today spiritualism is having tremendous vogue; men and women are getting into communication with departed spirits and putting themselves in league with the unseen powers. If you have got as far as reading fortunes in tea cups, stop. If you have gone as far as telling fortunes by cards, stop. I will tell you why—the devil uses these apparently harmless things to create a fearful curiosity in the minds of men and women, especially young men and women, and it may bring them into league with the angelic forces that hate God, into league with the principalities and the rulers of this world's darkness. Never say, "What is the harm in it?" Push it to its logical conclusion and ask, "Where will this end?" You are absolutely safe as long as you remain under the shelter of the Atonement; but if you do not—I don't care what your experiences are—you are absolutely unsafe. At any minute dangers may beset you, terrors and darkness may take hold of you and rack your life with terrific perils.

God grant we may keep as far away from these things as we can. But if in the strange providence of God you find you are near a spiritualist meeting, pray, and keep on your praying, and you will paralyze every power of the medium if he is genuine. No spiritualistic seance can continue if there is a Christian anywhere near who knows how to lay hold of God in prayer; no spirits will communicate. I could tell you wonderful stories of how God's power has worked. Blessed be God; Jesus Christ's salvation makes us more than conquerors over the angelic forces.

Majesties of the Unseen Universe

nor principalities. A *principality* is the jurisdiction of a prince. According to the Bible, the kingdoms of this world are under the rule of the prince of this world, namely, Satan (cf. Matthew 4:8–9). A time is coming when they will be taken from him—"the kingdoms of this world have become the kingdoms of our Lord and of His Christ" (Revelation 11:15), but at present they are in the devil's power.

Men say, "I can't help committing sin; I can't help doing this thing." Are they right? Perfectly right. You may talk further about a weak will; there is nothing more absurd. It is not the man's weak will; he has got into league with a power stronger than he is, and when a man gets in league with the prince of this world, I defy all his strength of will to stand before the terrific power of this world's darkness for one second. According to the New Testament, there is such a thing as obsession by unclean, malicious, wicked spirits who will damn and ruin body and soul in hell (cf. Luke 11:21–26). A moral empty heart is the resort of these spirits when a man is off his guard. But if a man has been born again of the Spirit of God and is keeping in the light, he cannot help going right because he is backed by the tremendous power of almighty God. What does the apostle John say?—"the wicked one does not touch him" (1 John 5:18). What a marvelous certainty! God grant we may be so filled with the Holy Spirit that we listen to His checks along every line. No power can deceive a child of God who keeps in the light with God. I am perfectly certain that the devil likes to deceive us and limit us in our practical belief as to what Jesus Christ can do. There is no limit to what He can do—absolutely none. "All things are possible to him who believes." (Mark 9:23). Jesus says that faith in Him is omnipotent. God grant we may get hold of this truth.

Miracles of the Unseen Universe

nor powers. The word is the same as that translated "miracles." A *miracle* is a work done by one who has fuller knowledge and authority than we have. Things that were called miracles a hundred years ago are not thought of as miracles today because men have come to a fuller knowledge. The miracles of Jesus were an exhibition of the power of God; that is, they were simply mirrors of what God Almighty is doing gradually and everywhere and all the time. And every miracle Jesus performed had a tremendous lesson behind it. It was not merely an exhibition of the power of God, there was always a moral meaning behind for the individual. That is why God does not heal some people. We are apt to confine life to one phase only, the physical; there are three phases: physical, psychical, and spiritual. Whenever Jesus touched the physical domain a miracle happened in the other phases as well. If a miracle is wrought by any other power in the physical it leaves no corresponding stamp of truth in the other domains of soul and spirit. In this dispensation it is not a question of whether God will sovereignly permit us to be delivered from sin, it is His express will that we should be delivered from sin; when it comes to healing it is not a question of God's will, but of His sovereignty, that is, whether the predispensational efficacy of the Atonement is active on our behalf just now. There is no case of healing in the Bible that did not come from a direct intervention of the sovereign touch of God. We make the mistake of putting an abstract truth deduced from the Word of God in the place of God Himself. When God does not heal it is time we got down to close quarters with Him and asked Him why. There is a deep lesson behind; we cannot lay down a general law for everyone, we can only find out the reason by going to God.

Our Lord revealed that the public power of Satan would be greater in the days in which we live than ever before. "For false christs and false prophets will rise, and show great signs and wonders to deceive, if possible, even the elect" (Matthew 24:24), and the apostle Paul foretold that there would be signs and lying wonders according to the working of Satan (see 2 Thessalonians 2:8–12), but we have no need to fear if we are experiencing the salvation of the Lord Jesus. He will banish all the tremendous powers and majesties that have been set against Him: "Having disarmed principalities and powers, He made a public spectacle of them, triumphing over them in it" (Colossians 2:15). According to the Bible, the One who laughs last is God. "He who sits in the heavens shall laugh" (Psalm 2:4). The apostle Paul has embraced every possible phase of the enemy's tactics, and he says we are more than conquerors in them all through Him who loved us.

The Frontier Battle Lines

> For I am persuaded that neither . . . things present nor things
> to come, nor height nor depth, nor any other created thing,
> shall be able to separate us from the love of God which is in
> Christ Jesus our Lord. (Romans 8:38–39)

In these verses Paul does not mention the ordinary trials of
life; he mentions the imperilling experiences that thousands have
gone through these past years, distress and anguish that hold the
eyes too much awake to sleep, tribulation that tears and lacerates
everything; but, he says, the love of God is untouched by these
experiences. That love renders impotent the strength of our most
formidable enemy. Any of the elemental ministries—life, death,
things present, things to come—may kill the castles built by
human love, may remove and shatter them like an incoming tide;
their strength is overwhelming, but they are powerless to touch
the love of God in Christ Jesus. When one reads the apostle Paul,
language seems completely beggared in the attempt to express his
devotion to Jesus Christ. Faith itself, with Paul, seems to be lost
sight of and merged altogether in his personal intimacy with Jesus
Christ; his is the very faith of the Son of God, which is not
conscious of itself. Remember, this is not meant only for the
apostle Paul, it is for everyone of us. God grant that the Holy
Spirit may so kindle all our natural powers, so invade us with the
power of God, that we may begin to "comprehend with all the
saints what is the width and length and depth and height"
(Ephesians 3:18) of the love of Christ for our souls.

The Infinitely Great

nor height. For generations the telescope has been made the
means of terrifying us instead of bringing God nearer to us. Those
who deal with the great secrets of the universe imply that our
planet is such a tiny spot in the tremendous universe that it is a
piece of stupid conceit on our part to think that God watches

over us. And to make our planet the center where God performed the marvelous drama of His own history of the Incarnation and Atonement is absurd, they say. But watch a simple-minded person, one who is right with God and is not terrified by the reasonings of men, as he looks at the stars and exclaims: "When I consider Your heavens, the work of Your fingers, the moon and the stars, which You have ordained, what is man that You are mindful of him?" (Psalm 8:3–4). It is said not in despair, but in adoring wonder. Then watch the man who is not right with God. The sight of the infinitely great to him pushes God right out of it, until God becomes a great first cause, a remote, cold principle. The far-flung battle lines reach beyond the stars to the very throne of God and deeper down than the deepest depths of hell; they may test and storm, they may spread seas and space, but, says Paul, "I am persuaded that they are not able to separate us from the love of God which is in Christ Jesus our Lord."

The Infinitely Little

nor depth. Look at the world through either a telescope or a microscope and you will be dwarfed into terror by the infinitely great or the infinitely little. Naturalists tell us that there are no two blades of grass alike, and close inspection of a bee's wing under a microscope reveals how marvelously it is made. What do I read in the Bible? I read that the God of heaven counts the hairs of our heads. Jesus says so. I read that the mighty God watches the sparrows so intimately that not one of them falls on the ground without His notice. I read that the God who holds the seas in the hollow of His hand and guides the stars in their courses clothes the grass of the field. Through the love of God in Christ Jesus we are brought into a wonderful intimacy with the infinitely great and the infinitely little.

The Infinitely Possible

nor any other creation. The apostle Paul knew better than most of us that there are principalities and powers and ordinances behind the seen universe that may at any moment flash forth as an uncanny, spiritual airship, or burst up from the deep as a terrific, supernatural submarine, terrifying us out of our wits. But, he says, no matter what the different creations may be, "I am persuaded that neither . . . height nor depth, nor any other created thing, shall be able to separate us from the love of God which is in Christ Jesus our Lord." Paul is not boasting; he is speaking from his own absolute certainty that the Cross of Christ has in it the very, secret, heart of God. We belittle and misrepresent the love of God when we see it merely on the surface. It is easy to think imperially, easy to think big thoughts and dream big dreams. But Jesus Christ is not big thoughts and big dreams. He is a tremendously big Savior for little insignificant creatures such as we are. Through the Atonement, God Almighty can place you, my poor, weak, timid, sin-tossed brother or sister, where nothing can touch you or harm you. No wonder the apostle Paul goes down to the lowest depths and climbs to the highest heights, and shouts in triumph—"we are more than conquerors through Him who loved us!"

If this great God is ours, what about our bodies; can He keep them in trim? What about our minds; can He keep our imaginations stayed upon Him so that we are able to say without hysterics, "Therefore we will not fear, even though the earth be removed, and though the mountains be carried into the midst of the sea" (Psalm 46:2)? Every now and again an attack from the unseen realm may surprise us and take us off our guard, but if we are right with God, what do we find? We find God on guard, and we are amazed and stand back and say, "Why, this is wonderful!"—"kept by the power of God" (1 Peter 1:5).

"Who shall separate us from the love of Christ?" At the end of all trials, and when there is no more trial, the love of God is not finished; it still goes on: "having loved His own who were in the world, He loved them to the end" (John 13:1). This is the great theme that keeps the soul of the saint undaunted in courage. It does not matter where a man may get to in the way of tribulation or anguish, none of it can wedge in between and separate him from the love of God in Christ Jesus.

Consider this simple illustration. Children are sometimes afraid in the dark, fear gets into their hearts and nerves and they get into a tremendous state; then they hear the voice of mother or father, and all is quieted and they go off to sleep. In our own spiritual experience it is the same: some terror comes down the road to meet us and our hearts are seized with a tremendous fear; then we hear our own names called and the voice of Jesus saying, "It is I, do not be afraid" (Matthew 14:27), and the peace of God that surpasses all understanding takes possession of our hearts.

The Soul of a Christian

Soul Satisfaction

O LORD, You have searched me and known me. (Psalm 139:1)

None of them can by any means redeem his brother, nor give to God a ransom for him—for the redemption of their souls is costly, and it shall cease forever. (Psalm 49:7–8)

Beware of believing that the human soul is simple, for it is not true. Read Psalm 139, and look into yourself, and you will soon find you are much too complex to touch. Charles Wagner was the apostle of naturalness—the gospel of temperament—be simple! How can anyone who is wide-awake be simple? We befool ourselves into moral imbecility if we believe those who tell us the human soul is simple. As long as we think we understand ourselves we are in a lamentable state of ignorance. The first dose of conviction of sin or of the realization of what the psalmist states, namely, the unfathomable depths of our own souls, will put an end to that ignorance. The only One who can redeem the human soul is the Lord Jesus Christ and He has done it, and the Holy Spirit brings the realization of this to us experimentally. All this vast complex "me," which we cannot begin to understand, God knows completely, and through the Atonement He invades every part of the personality with His life.

Soul is the responsible expression of the ruling personal spirit, and when the personal spirit is filled with God's Spirit, we have to see that we obey His Spirit and reconstruct the soul.

God's Spirit entering my spirit does not become my spirit, but quickens my spirit, and I begin to express a new soul. It is not the nature of the working of the soul that is altered; that remains the same in a regenerate human spirit as in an unregenerate human spirit. But a different driving power expresses itself. When God's Spirit comes into my personal spirit, instantly I am introduced to a life that manifests itself in contradiction to my old way of reasoning and expressing myself, and the consequence is that the life whereby I have affinity with other people is upset and they wonder what is the matter with me; a disturbing element has come in that cannot be estimated. The incoming of the Spirit of God disturbs the reasoning faculties, and for a while the soul that is born from above is inarticulate, it has no expression; the equilibrium has been upset by the incoming of a totally new spirit into my spirit, and Jesus Christ says, "By your patience possess your souls" (Luke 21:19)—acquire your renewed soul with patience.

Satisfaction and the demand for satisfaction is a God-given principle in human nature, but it must be satisfaction in the highest. "Blessed are those who hunger and thirst for righteousness; for they shall be filled" (Matthew 5:6).

Naturally

> But the natural man does not receive the things of the Spirit of God, for they are foolishness to him; nor can he know them, because they are spiritually discerned. (1 Corinthians 2:14)

We preach to men as if they were conscious they were dying sinners. They are not; they are having a good time, and our talk about being born from above is in a domain they know nothing of. We do not need the Holy Spirit to reveal that immorality is wrong, but we do need the Holy Spirit to reveal that the complacency of the natural life has Satan at its basis. Nowadays we have come to the conclusion that a man must be a down-and-out sinner before he needs Jesus Christ to do anything for him; consequently we debase Jesus Christ's salvation to mean merely that He can save the vile and sensual man and lift him into a better life. We quote our Lord's statement that "the Son of Man has come to seek and to save that which was lost" (Luke 19:10) and misinterpret His meaning by limiting *the lost* to those who are lost in our eyes.

The natural man does not want to be born again. If a man's morality is well within his own grasp and he has enough religion to give the right tone to his natural life, to talk about being born again seems utterly needless. The natural man is not in distress, he is not conscious of conviction of sin, or of any disharmony; he is quite contented and at peace. Conviction of sin is the realization that my natural life is based on a disposition that will not have Jesus Christ. The gospel does not present what the natural man wants, but what he needs, and the gospel awakens an intense resentment as well as an intense craving. We will take God's blessings and loving-kindnesses and prosperities, but when it comes to the need of having our disposition altered, there is opposition at once. When we come down to close quarters and God's Spirit tells us we must give up the right to ourselves to Jesus Christ and let Him rule, then we understand what Paul meant when he said that "the carnal mind," which resides in the heart, is "enmity against God" (Romans 8:7 KJV).

No man can have his state of mind altered without suffering for it in his body, and that is why men do anything to avoid conviction of sin. When a worldly man who is happy, moral and upright comes in contact with Jesus Christ, his "beauty," that is, the perfectly ordered completeness of his nature, is destroyed and that man must be persuaded that Jesus Christ has a better kind of life for him, otherwise he feels he had better not have come across Him. If I knew nothing about sin before the Holy Spirit came, then why did He come? If I am peaceful and happy and contented and living my life with my morality well within my own grasp, why does the Holy Spirit need to come in and upset the balance and make me miserable and unfit for anything? It is time we asked ourselves these questions. God's Book gives us the answer. Thank God, we are coming to the end of the shallow presentation of Christianity that makes out that Jesus Christ came only to give us peace. Thousands of people are happy without God in this world, but that kind of happiness and peace is on a wrong level. Jesus Christ came to send a sword through every peace that is not based on a personal relationship to Him. He came to put us right with God that His own peace might reign.

Satanically

> But even if our gospel is veiled, it is veiled to those who are perishing whose minds the god of this age has blinded, who do not believe, lest the light of the gospel of the glory of Christ, who is the image of God, should shine on them. (2 Corinthians 4:3–4)

Paul did not say *the perishing,* were the drunkards and social pariahs, but those "whose minds the god of this age has blinded, who do not believe"—they see nothing whatever in all that Jesus Christ stands for

If the natural remains united with itself long enough it will lead to a deadly, satanic satisfaction, a blind happiness. The words *diabolical* and *satanic* do not mean the same. Judas became diabolical: "the devil having already put it into the heart of Judas Iscariot, Simon's son, to betray Him" (John 13:2); Peter became satanic: "But He turned and said to Peter, 'Get behind Me, Satan!' " (Matthew 16:23). When our Lord came face-to-face with Satan He dealt with him as representing the attitude man takes up in organizing his life apart from any consideration of God. For a thing to be satanic does not mean that it is abominable and immoral; the satanically managed man is absolutely self-governed and has no need of God.

When Satan rules the hearts of natural men under the inspiration of the devil, they are not troubled, they are at peace, entrenched in clean worldliness (cf. Psalm 73); before God can rule a man's kingdom He must first overthrow this false rule. In the parable in Luke 11:21 our Lord says that "when a strong man, fully armed [Satan], guards his own palace, his goods [i.e., the souls of men] are in peace"; there is no breaking out into sin and wrongdoing. The one thing the prince of this world will guard against is the incoming of Jesus Christ, the "stronger than he," because "he takes from him all his armor in which he trusted" (verse 22). The coming of Jesus Christ is not a peaceful thing, it is a disturbing, an overwhelming thing. Am I willing to be born into the realm Jesus Christ is in? If so, I must be prepared for chaos straight off in the realm I am in. The rule that has come in between God and man has to be eclipsed, and Jesus Christ's entering in means absolute chaos concerning the way I have been looking at things, a turning of everything upside down. "Do not think that I come to bring peace on earth. I did not come to bring peace but a sword" (Matthew 10:34). The old order and the old peace must go, and we cannot get back peace on the old level. As soon as Jesus Christ comes in that peace is gone, and instead there is the sword of conviction. A man does not need the Holy Spirit to tell him that external sins are wrong, ordinary culture and education will do that; but it does take the Holy Spirit to convict us of sin as our Lord defined it. The Holy Spirit is unmistakable in His working, and our Lord said that, "When He has come, He will convict the world of sin, . . . because they do not believe in Me" (John 16:8–9). That is the very essence of sin. If we have allowed Jesus Christ to upset the equilibrium, holiness is the inevitable result, or no peace forever.

One of the most cunning travesties of Satan is to say that he is the instigator of drunkenness and external sins. Man himself is responsible for doing wrong things, and he does wrong things because of the wrong disposition that is in him. The true blame for sin lies in the wrong disposition, and the cunning of our nature makes us blame Satan when we should blame ourselves. When men go into external sins Satan is probably as much upset as the Holy Spirit, but for a different reason. Satan knows perfectly well that when men go into external sin and upset their lives, they will want another Ruler, a Savior, a Deliverer; but as long as he can keep them in peace and unity and harmony apart from God he will do so. The Bible reveals that there is a solidarity of sin, a bond of union that keeps men together, known as "the body of sin"; it is the mutual inheritance of the human race (see Romans 5:12). The Bible also reveals that Satan is anxious to keep that solidarity intact because whenever men break out into immoral conduct, it disintegrates his kingdom. The one other force that disintegrates the solidarity of sin is the Spirit of God. Never have the idea that a worldling is unhappy; a worldling is perfectly happy, as thoroughly happy as a Christian. The persons who are unhappy are the worldlings or the Christians if they are not at one with the principle that binds them. When a worldling is not a worldling at heart, he is miserable, and when a Christian is not a Christian at heart, he is miserable; he carries his religion like a headache instead of something that is worth having. Remember then, the two things that disintegrate Satan's kingdom—breaking out into acts of sin and conviction by the Spirit of God. This is the solution of a number of moral problems

The beginning of calamities from the natural standpoint is when our Lord comes across people. The thing that upsets our natural complacency is a touch from our Lord. It may come in a personal interview (as in John 4), but when it comes it is all up instantly with the old order, we can never get it back. Before the Spirit of God can bring peace of mind He has to clear out the rubbish, and before He can do that He has to give us an idea of what rubbish there is.

Spiritually

> But God . . . even when we were dead in trespasses, made us alive together with Christ (by grace you have been saved), and raised us up together, and made us sit together in the heavenly places in Christ Jesus. (Ephesians 2:4–6)

If all Jesus Christ came to do was to upset me, make me unfit for my work, upset my friendships and my life, produce disturbance and misery and distress, then I wish He had never come. But that is not all He came to do. He came to lift us up to the heavenly places where He is Himself. The whole claim of the redemption of Jesus is that He can satisfy the last aching abyss of the human soul, not hereafter only, but here and now. Satisfaction does not mean stagnation, it means the knowledge that we have the right type of life for our souls. The hymn has it rightly, "Oh, the peace my Savior gives!" That peace is the deepest thing a human personality can know; it is almighty. The apostle Paul emphasizes the hilarity of life—"Do not be drunk with wine . . . but be filled with the Spirit" (Ephesians 5:18). Enthusiasm is the idea, intoxicated with the life of God. The healthy pagan and the healthy saint are the ones described in God's Book as hilarious; all in between are diseased and more or less sick. We have no business to be sick unless it is just a preparatory stage toward something better, when God is nursing us through some spiritual illness; but if it is the main characteristic of the life there is something wrong.

"Blessed are the poor in spirit" (Matthew 5:3). The knowledge of our own poverty brings us to the moral frontier where Jesus Christ works; then He says, If you ask God, He will give you the Holy Spirit. "If you then, being evil, know how to give good gifts to your children, how much more will your heavenly Father give the Holy Spirit to those who ask Him?" (Luke 11:13). The Holy Spirit is the One who regenerates us into the kingdom to which Jesus Christ belongs. "Do not marvel that I said to you, 'You must be born again' " (John 3:7). The touch that comes is as mysterious as the wind. The miracle of the creation of redemption in our souls is that we suddenly feel an insatiable desire for salvation. Our Lord said, "No one can come to Me unless the Father who sent Me draws him" (John 6:44), and that is the way He draws him. Redemption is the great reality that is continually creating within us a longing for God.

The Soul of a Christian   155

God's Searching of a Sincere Soul

Intercessory Introspection

> Search me, O God, and know my heart; try me, and know
> my anxieties. (Psalm 139:23)

It is far more rare to find a sincere soul than one might suppose. No one but a fool or a sincere soul would ever pray this prayer; "Search me, O God," search me right out to the remotest depths, to the innermost recesses of my thoughts and imaginations; scrutinize me through and through until I know that You know me utterly, that I may be saved from my own ways and brought into Your way. Any soul who prays that prayer will be answered.

Psalm 139 states for us the profoundest experience of a soul's life with God. It is a marvelous moment in a man's life when he knows he is explored by God. The introspective tendency in us that makes us want to examine ourselves and know the springs of our thoughts and motives takes the form of prayer with the psalmist. He speaks of God as the Creator of the vast universe outside him, of God's omnipotence and omnipresence, but he does not end there. There is something infinitely more mysterious to the psalmist than the universe outside him and that is the mystery of his own soul. "There are mountain peaks in my soul I cannot climb, ocean depths I cannot fathom; there are possibilities within that terrify me, therefore, O God, search me." That is introspective intercession.

We must live scrutinized by God, and if you want to know what the scrutiny of God is like, listen to Jesus Christ: "for from within, out of the heart of men, proceed evil thoughts" (Mark 7:21), and then follows a rugged catalog of things few of us know anything about in conscious life; consequently we are apt to be indignant and resent Jesus Christ's diagnosis: "I have never felt like a murderer or an adulterer, therefore those things cannot be in me." To talk in that way is proof that we are grossly ignorant of ourselves. If we prefer to trust our ignorant innocence we pass a verdict on the only Master of the human heart there is; we tell Him He does not know what He is talking about. The one right thing to do is to listen to Jesus Christ and then hand our hearts over to God to be searched and guarded and filled with the Holy Spirit, then the wonderful thing is that we never need know and never shall know in actual experience the truth of Jesus Christ's revelation about the human heart. But if we stand on our own rights and wisdom, at any second an eruption may occur in our personal lives and we shall discover to our unutterable horror that what Jesus said is appallingly true.

We have no business to be ignorant about ourselves. If any of us have come to manhood or womanhood with the idea that we have a holy innocence on the inside, we are desperately deluded. There is no human being on earth with an innocence that is not based on ignorance, and if we have come to the stage of life we are now in with the belief that innocence and purity are the same thing, it is because we have paid no attention to what Jesus Christ said. Purity is something that has been tested and tried and has triumphed; innocence has always to be shielded. When the Holy Spirit comes in, He brings into the center of the personal life the very Spirit that was manifested in the life of the Lord Jesus, namely, the Holy Spirit. Jesus Christ has undertaken through His redemption to put into us a heart so pure that God Almighty can see nothing to censure in it, and the Holy Spirit searches us not only to make us know the possibilities of iniquity in our hearts, but to make us unblameable in holiness in His sight.

The great cry today is, "Fulfill yourself, work out what is in you." If you do, you will work out your own condemnation. But if you let God deal with what is wrong, let Him presence you with Divinity, you will be able to work out what He works in, which is a totally different thing. The cry to realize ourselves is the cry to keep God out. If we do not know the tremendous depths of possible iniquity in our hearts, it is because we have never been scrutinized by the Holy Spirit, but let Him turn His searchlight right down to the inmost recesses and the best of us are shuddering on our faces before God. When the Holy Spirit does scrutinize us (and He will not do it if we do not want Him to, this is the day of our option; a time is coming when He will do it whether we want Him to or not, when we will be only too glad to creep anywhere out of the sight of God whose eyes search as a flame of fire), He reveals not only a depth of possible iniquity that makes us shudder, but a height of holiness of which we never dreamed. The great, mystic work of the Holy Spirit is in the dim regions of our personalities where we cannot go: "And may your whole spirit, soul and body be preserved blameless at the coming of our Lord Jesus Christ" (1 Thessalonians 5:23). But no man can get there! Then, was the apostle Paul mad when he said we could be presented "holy and blameless and above reproach in His sight" (Colossians 1:22)? No, the apostle Paul had been to the Cross of Christ and had learned there a secret that made him say, "God forbid that I should boast except in the cross of our Lord Jesus Christ" (Galatians 6:14), because it is by means of His Cross that Jesus Christ can present us faultless before the throne of God. "Do you mean to say that God can bring the winnowing fan of His Spirit and search out my thoughts and imaginations and find nothing deserving of blame?" That is the meaning of the Atonement as far as our practical experience is concerned; no soul gets there except by the sovereign grace of God. If we have not caught the meaning of the tremendous moral aspect of the Atonement it is because we have never prayed this prayer, "Search me, O God." Are we sincere enough to ask God to search us and sincere enough to abide by what His searching reveals?

Impeccable Integrity

> But if we walk in the light as He is in the light, . . . the blood
> of Jesus Christ His Son cleanses us from all sin. (1 John 1:7)

If that means cleansing from all sin in conscious experience only, may God have mercy on us. A man who has been made obtuse by sin will say he is not conscious of sin. Cleansing from all sin by the blood of Jesus is far deeper than we can be conscious of; it is cleansing from all sin in the sight of God because the disposition of His Son is working out in every particular, not to our consciousness, but deeper than our consciousness. We are not cleansed more and more from all sin; if we walk in the light, as God is in the light, we are cleansed from all sin. In our consciousness it works with a keen, poignant knowledge of what sin is. The great need today among those of us who profess sanctification is the patience and ability to work out the holiness of God in every detail of our lives. When we are first adjusted to God the Holy Spirit works on the big general lines; then He begins to educate us down to the scruple, He makes us sensitive over things we never before thought of. No matter what our experience may be we must beware of the curse of being stationary, we have to go on and on "perfecting holiness in the fear of God" (2 Corinthians 7:1).

If you have been making a great profession in your religious life but begin to find that the Holy Spirit is scrutinizing you, let His searchlight go straight down, and He will not only search you, He will put everything right that is wrong; He will make the past as though it had never been; He will "restore to you the years that the swarming locust has eaten" (Joel 2:25); He will blot out the "handwriting of requirements" that is against you (Colossians 2:14); He will put His Spirit within you and cause you to walk in His ways; He will make you pure in the deepest recesses of your personality. Thank God, Jesus Christ's salvation is a flesh-and-blood reality!

Who is going to do all this in us? The Lord Jesus Christ. Let Jesus Christ proclaim His gospel: we can have the very disposition of Jesus imparted to us, and if we have not got it we will have to tell God the reason why. We have to tell God we don't believe He can do it—there are details of our lives He cannot put right, back tracks He cannot clear up, ramifications of evil He cannot touch. Thank God that is a lie! He can. If God cannot do that, we have "followed cunningly devised fables" (2

Peter 1:16). That is where the fight has to be fought—along the line of what Jesus Christ can do in the human soul. Unless God has searched us and cleansed us and filled us with the Holy Spirit so that we are undeserving of censure in His sight, the Atonement has not been applied to our personal experience.

Are we willing to let God scrutinize us, or are we doing that worst of all things, trying to justify ourselves? People say if they are living up to all the light they have, meaning the light of conscience, they are all right. We may be consciously free of sin, but we are not justified on that account; we may be walking in the light of conscience, but we are not justified on that account either (cf. 1 Corinthians 4:3–4); we are only justified in the sight of God through the Atonement at work in our inner lives. God grant we may let His searching scrutiny go right through us until there is nothing He has not searched. We are far too big for ourselves, infinitely too big. The majority of us try to put ourselves in a bandbox, but we cannot cabin and confine our lives. There is a purpose in every life that is in God's keeping, of which we know little but which He will fulfill if we let Him rightly relate us to Himself.

The Need To Be a Christian

Never confuse personality with consciousness. Personality is the perplexing factor of myself that continually changes and yet remains the same. All we can deal with in psychology is consciousness, but God does not limit our salvation by our consciousness. The need to be a Christian is not simply that Jesus Christ's salvation may work in the conscious life, but that the unconscious realm of the personality may be protected from supernatural powers of which we know nothing. When the Holy Spirit enters into us He brings the marvelous revelation that God guards the unfathomable part of our personalities; He goes to the springs of our personal lives that we cannot touch and prevents our being tampered with and bewitched out of God's purpose in redemption. We belittle and misrepresent the redemption if we refer it merely to the conscious life. Many spiritual testimonies get as far as: "Once I was that in conscious life, and now I am this, and Jesus did it." Well, thank God for that, but we are much more than we are conscious of, and if Jesus Christ only came to alter the conscious life, then the redemption is much ado about nothing. But when we come to examine the New Testament we find that redemption does infinitely more than alter our conscious lives; it safeguards the unconscious realm that we cannot touch. Our conscious experience is simply the doorway into the only reality there is, namely, the redemption. We are not only presenced with Divinity, but protected by Deity in the depths of personality below the conscious realm.

Practical Invasions from the Unconscious

Part of the personal life is conscious, but the greater part is unconscious; every now and again the unconscious part emerges into the conscious and upsets us because we do not know where it comes from or where it leads to, and we get afraid of ourselves. There is a great deal more of "me" I do not know than that I do know. No man knows the springs of his motives or of his will; when we begin to examine ourselves we come to the threshold of the unconscious and cannot go any further. The psalmist realized this when he prayed, "Search me, O God"; explore me to the beginning of my motives. Below the threshold of consciousness is the subconscious part of our personalities which is full of mystery. There are forces in this realm that may interfere with us and we cannot control them; it is with this realm that the Spirit of God deals.

An island of the sea is easily explored, yet it may prove to be but the top of a mountain, the greater part of which is hidden under the sea, going down to deeper depths than we can fathom. So our personalities are infinitely more than we can be conscious of; consequently we must never estimate ourselves by the part we are conscious of or be so stupid as to say we are only what we are conscious of. We are all in danger of doing this until we come across things in ourselves that surprise us. People say, "Oh, I can't understand myself!" Of course you cannot. "No one else understands me!" Of course they don't; if they did, you would not be worth understanding. There is only one Being who understands us, and that is our Creator. We must beware of estimating God's salvation by our experience of it. Our experience is a mere indication in conscious life of an almighty salvation that goes far beyond anything we ever can experience.

Have we ever awakened to the fact that there are forces of evil around us greater than we can control? Jesus Christ by His redemption not only saves us completely, but keeps us oblivious of the awful dangers there are outside: "the wicked one does not touch him" (1 John 5:18). We are kept where we are unconscious of the need to be kept. Thank God for His safeguarding, for His salvation that keeps us, waking and sleeping, conscious and unconscious, in danger and out of it.

There are supernatural powers and agencies that can play with us like toys whenever they choose unless we are garrisoned by God. The New Testament continually impresses this upon us: "For we do not wrestle against flesh and blood, but against principalities, against powers, against the rulers of the darkness of this age, against spiritual hosts of wickedness in the heavenly places" (Ephesians 6:12). According to the Bible, spiritualism is not a trick, it is a fact. Man can communicate with beings of a different order from his own; he can put himself into a state of subjectivity in which spirits can appear. A medium commits the great crime psychically because he gives himself over to a force the nature of which he does not know. He does great violence to his own rectitude and tampers with the balance of his sanity by putting himself into league with powers the character of which he does not know. Mediumship, whereby unseen spirits talk to men and women, will destroy the basis of moral sanity because it introduces a man into domains he had better leave alone. Drunkenness and debauchery are child's play compared with the peril of spiritualism. There is something uncannily awful about tampering with these supernatural powers, and in the speeding up of these days the necromantic element is increasing. Be on the lookout for the manifestations that are not of God; all have the one sign, they ignore Jesus Christ. Beware of the advice, "Yield, give up your will." No man or woman has any right to yield to any impression or any influence; as soon as anyone does he or she is susceptible to all kinds of supernatural powers. There is only one Being to whom we must yield, and that is the Lord Jesus Christ. Be sure that it is Jesus Christ to whom you yield, then the whole nature is safeguarded for ever.

Pushing Down God's Barriers

When the Holy Spirit comes in He makes us know that there are things we must remain ignorant of. Beware of entering into competition with the Holy Spirit. When we become curious and pry where we have no business to pry, we are eating of the fruit of the tree of which God said, "You shall not eat" of it (see Genesis 2:17). The spiritualistic trend of today is an example of this very thing. Men and women are pushing down God's barriers and coming into contact with forces they cannot control. Unless we hand over the keeping of our personalities to God to garrison, there are a hundred and one influences that can come into us that we never can control but which will soon control us. The blight of God rests on a man or woman who dares to take any way of knowing what is hidden other than Jesus Christ's way. He is the only One who is "worthy to open the scroll" (Revelation 5:2). If by intellectual curiosity we push away the barriers God has seen fit to put, we shall experience pain and suffering from which God will not protect us. We cannot play the fool with our bodies and souls and hoodwink God. Certain kinds of moral disobedience produce sicknesses that no physical remedy can touch; the only cure is obedience to Jesus Christ. The barriers are placed by a God who is absolutely holy, and He has told us clearly, "Not that way." If we turn to necromancy even in such seemingly ridiculous ways

The Soul of a Christian 163

of telling fortunes in teacups or by cards or planchette, we commit a crime against our own souls, we are probing where we have no right to probe. People say, "There's no harm in it." There is all the harm and the backing up of the devil in it. The only One who can open up the profound mysteries of life is God, and He will do it as He sees we can stand it (cf. Deuteronomy 29:29).

Soul is the expression of the personal spirit in the body, and it is the expression of soul that is either good or bad. What we do tells as much as what we are in the final issue. There are two entrances into the soul: the body and the spirit. The body is within our control, the spirit is not, and if the spirit is not under the control of God there is nothing to prevent other spirits communicating through it to the soul and body. It is impossible to guard the spirit; the only One who can guard its entrances is God. If we hand ourselves over to His keeping we shall be kept not only from what we understand as dangers, but from dangers we have never even imagined. The conscious ring of the life is a mere phase; Jesus Christ did not die to save that only; it is the whole personality that is included in the redemption. We are safeguarded from dangers we know nothing about. Thank God if the unseen realm does not impinge on you. There are people in whom the walls between the seen and unseen are exceedingly thin and they are constantly being tortured; the salvation of Jesus Christ can save them from it all. We are ill taught if we look for results only in the earthlies when we pray. A praying saint performs far more havoc among the unseen forces of darkness than we have the slightest notion of.

Perils of Self-ignorance

> Who can understand his errors? Cleanse me from secret faults. (Psalm 19:12)

Is there some fault God has been checking you about and you have left it alone? Be careful lest it end in a dominant sin. The errors are silent, they creep in on us, and when we stand in the light of Jesus Christ we are amazed to find the conclusions we have come to. The reason is that we have deluded ourselves. This self-security keeps us entirely ignorant of what we really are, ignorant of the things that make the salvation of Jesus Christ necessary. When we say to ourselves, "Oh well, I am no worse than anyone else," that is the beginning; we shall soon produce blindness to our own defects and entrench ourselves around with a fictitious security. Jesus Christ has no chance whatever with the man who has the silent security of self-ignorance. When such a man hears anyone speak about deliverance from sin, he is untouched—"I have no need to be delivered." Paul says, "If our gospel is veiled, it is veiled to those . . . whose minds the god of this age has blinded" (2 Corinthians 4:3–4), blinded to everything Jesus Christ stands for, and a man is to blame for getting there.

For a man to be at peace in his mind, undisturbed, and at unity in himself is a good thing, because in a united personality there is freedom from self-consciousness; but if that peace and unity are without any consideration of Jesus Christ, it is a peace of death, a peace altogether apart from God, and when the Holy Spirit comes in He comes not as a Comforter, but as a thorough Disturber and upsets this natural unity. No wonder men will do anything to avoid conviction of sin, anything to keep the searchlight of God out, anything to keep away from morbid introspection. But thank God for the men and women who have come to the end of themselves and who say, "Search me, O God," I cannot live any longer in a vain show; and He will do it. We are driven back every time to our relationship with God; it is the only safe thing.

If the Spirit of God can come into the unconscious part of our personalities, the spirit of the devil can come there also. "The devil having already put it into the heart of Judas Iscariot [the personality of Judas] . . . to betray Him" (John 13:2), and Jesus said of Judas, " 'Did I not choose you, the twelve, and one of you is a devil?' He spoke of Judas Iscariot, the son of Simon" (John 6:70–71). Some people seem to think it is an amazingly clever

The Soul of a Christian   165

thing to doubt Jesus Christ; it is an evil thing. Whenever the evil personality of unbelief asked the Lord anything, He never answered; but when the heart cries out, He answers immediately.

"When He has come, He will convict . . . of sin, [because men are immoral? No] because they do not believe in Me" (John 16:8–9). These words reveal the very essence of sin. Sin is not measured by a creed or social order: sin is measured by a person, Jesus Christ. When the Holy Spirit comes in He is unmistakable in the direction of His work; He goes direct to the thing that keeps us from believing in Jesus Christ. The work of the Holy Spirit is to make us realize the meaning of the redemption. As long as we believe it on the outside it does not upset our complacency, but we don't want to be perturbed on the inside. Paul says that some people have "foolish hearts": "Although they knew God, they did not glorify Him as God" (Romans 1:21). In actual life they were amazingly shrewd and calculating, but their hearts were foolish toward God. Beware of turning your back on what you know is true because you do not want it to be real. Jesus Christ never says that a man is damned because he is a sinner; the condemnation is when a man sees what Jesus Christ came to do and will not let Him do it. That is the critical moment, "the condemnation," in a man's life (John 3:19).

There are possibilities below the threshold of our lives that no one knows but God. We cannot understand ourselves or know the springs of our motives; consequently our examination of ourselves can never be unbiased or unprejudiced. We are only safe in taking an estimate of ourselves from our Creator, not from our own introspection. But although introspection cannot profoundly satisfy us, we must not conclude that introspection is wrong. Introspection is right because it is the only way we shall discover that we need God. Introspection without God leads to insanity. The people who have no tendency to introspect are described as "dead in trespasses and sins" (Ephesians 2:1), quite happy, quite contented, quite moral. All they want is easily within their own grasp, but they are dead to the world to which Jesus

Christ belongs, and it takes His voice and His Spirit to awaken them. If we estimate life by the abundance of things that we possess consciously, there will come a drastic awakening one day because we shall have to leave it all at death. We shall have to leave this body, which keeps the personal spirit in conscious life, and go clean through the threshold of consciousness to where we do not know. It is a desperate thing to die if we have only been living in the conscious realm.

These aspects reveal the need to be a Christian as an enormous need. Thank God for the amazing security of His salvation! It keeps us not only in conscious life but from dangers of which we know nothing, unseen and hidden dangers, subtle and desperate.

Characteristics of the Soul

The Soul in Sinful Badness—Working Inward

Gross Inquisitiveness

> So when the woman saw that the tree was good for food,
> that it was pleasant to the eyes, and a tree desirable to make
> one wise, she took of its fruit and ate (Genesis 3:6)

There are some things of which we must be ignorant because knowledge of them comes in no other way than by disobedience to God. In the life originally designed for Adam it was not intended that he should be ignorant of evil, but that he should know evil through understanding good. Instead, he ate of the fruit of the tree of knowledge of good and evil and thereby knew evil positively and good negatively; consequently none of us knows the order God intended. The knowledge of evil that comes through the Fall has given human nature a bias of insatiable curiosity about the bad, and only when we have been introduced into the kingdom of God do we know good and evil in the way God constituted man to know them.

If we want to discover things in the material universe we must be intellectually curious; but for finding things out scientifically it does not matter whether a man is good or bad. It is right to be curious about the natural world; if we are not intellectually curious we shall never learn anything. God never encourages laziness. But when we come to the domain Jesus Christ lives in, curiosity is of no avail. The only way to find out things in the moral universe is by obedience.

The philosophy of life is based on the topsy-turvy reasoning of going into things in order to find out about them, which is like saying you have to go into the mud before you can know what clean water is. "I must know the world"—if you do, you will only know good by contrast with evil. Modern teaching implies that we must be grossly experienced before we are of any use in the world. That is not true. Jesus Christ knew good and evil by the life that was in Him, and God intended that man's knowledge of evil should come in the same way as to our Lord, namely, through the rigorous integrity of obedience to God. When a man is convicted of sin he knows how terrific is the havoc sin has wrought in him and he knows with what a mighty salvation he has been visited by God, but it is only by obedience to the Holy Spirit that he begins to know what an awful thing sin is.

A great deal of our social work today is a history of moral housebreaking; men and women have gone into work to which God never sent them, consequently their moral and spiritual integrity has been violated. Work is taken up with the absurd deification of pluck, "This thing has got to be done, and I must do it"—and they damage their souls in doing it because God is not there to protect. But when a man or woman is called of God, the facts he or she has to face never upset the equilibrium of the life because it is garrisoned by the presence of God. Too often when merely moral men or women go into bad surroundings they become soiled, no matter what their moral standard is, but the men and women who have been made pure by the Holy Spirit are kept like the light, unsullied.

Growing Iniquity

> And He said, . . . "Have you eaten from the tree of which I
> commanded you that you should not eat?" (Genesis 3:11;
> Jude 4, 10)

Every child born of natural generation is innocent, but it is
the innocence of ignorance. Naturally we are in an impaired state,
and when our innocence is turned into knowledge we find to our
humiliation how tremendously impaired it is. It is the ignorant
innocence of determinedly being without the knowledge of God
(Romans 1:18–23). It is safer to trust God's revelation than our
own innocence. Jesus Christ is either the supreme authority on the
human heart or He is not worth listening to, and He said: "From
within, out of the heart of men, proceed . . ." (Mark 7:21), and then
comes that very ugly catalog. Jesus did not say, "Into the human
heart these things are injected," but, "from within, out of the heart"
of men all these evil things proceed. If we trust our innocent
ignorance to secure us, it is likely that as life goes on there will
come a burst-up from underneath into the conscious life that will
reveal to us that we are uncommonly like what Jesus Christ said.

Iniquity means turning out of the straight. Whenever anything
begins to turn you out of the straight, stop and get it put right, no
matter what else suffers. If you don't, you will grow in iniquity, and
if you grow in iniquity you will call iniquity integrity, sensuality
spirituality, and, ultimately, the devil God. The most terrible verdict
on the human soul is that it no longer believes in purity, and no
man gets there without being himself to blame. There is such a
thing as "paradise lost." The gates can never again be opened in this
life; they are shut as inevitably as God shuts anything.

Great Independence

> Then the serpent said to the woman, "You will not surely
> die. For God knows that in the day you eat of it your eyes

will be opened, and you will be like God, knowing good and evil." (Genesis 3:4–5 see verse 22)

Adam was intended by God to take part in his own development by a series of moral choices, to sacrifice his natural life to God by obedience and thereby transform it into a spiritual life. Instead, he deliberately ate of the fruit of the tree of the knowledge of good and evil, and thereby became god over himself (Genesis 3:5). The characteristic of sin is independence of God: "I can look after myself; I know exactly how far to go. I intend to develop my life without God—why shouldn't I?" Whenever we say, "Why shouldn't I?" we tell Jesus Christ to retire and we take our lives into our own hands, and instead of working from within and manifesting the beauty of holiness, we work inward and become more and more self-centered, harder, and more indifferent to external things.

The knowledge of evil that came through the Fall gives a man a broad mind, but instead of instigating him to action it paralyzes his action. Men and women whose minds are poisoned by gross experience of evil are marvelously generous with regard to other people's sins; they argue in this way: "To know all is to pardon all." Every bit of their broadmindedness paralyzes their power to do anything. They know good only by contrast with evil, which is the exact opposite of God's order. When a man knows good and evil in the way God intended he should, he becomes intolerant of evil, and this intolerance shows itself in an intense activity against evil. Jesus Christ never tolerated sin for one moment, and when His nature is having its way in us the same intolerance is shown. The marvel of the grace of God is that He can take the strands of evil and twistedness out of a man's mind and imagination and make him simple toward God. Restoration through the redemption of Jesus Christ makes a man simple, and simplicity always shows itself in action. There is nothing simple in the human soul or in human life. The only simple thing is the relationship of the soul to Jesus Christ; that is why the apostle Paul says, "I fear, lest somehow, . . . your minds may be corrupted from the simplicity that is in Christ" (2 Corinthians 11:3).

The Soul in Spiritual Beauty—Working Outward

Golden Ignorance

> And the LORD God formed man of the dust of the ground, and breathed into his nostrils the breath of life; and man became a living being. (Genesis 2:7)

The presentation of true Christian experience brings us face-to-face with spiritual beauty, a beauty that can never be forced or imitated because it is a manifestation from within of a simple relationship to God that is being worked out all the time. There is nothing simple except a man's relation to God in Christ, and that relationship must never be allowed to be complicated. Our Lord's childhood expresses this spiritual beauty, "And the Child grew and became strong in spirit, filled with wisdom . . . . And Jesus increased in wisdom and stature" (Luke 2:40, 52). The great characteristic of our Lord's life was that of "golden ignorance"; there were things He did not know and that He refused to know. Jesus Christ developed in the way God intended human beings to develop, and He exhibited the kind of life we ought to live when we have been born from above. "But," you say, "how am I to live a life like Jesus Christ? I have not the 'golden ignorance' He had; I have a heredity I had no say in, I am not holy nor likely to be." The marvel of the redemption is that Jesus Christ can put into any man His own hereditary disposition of holiness, and all the standards He gives are based on that disposition. "Do not marvel that I said to you, 'You must be born again' " (John 3:7). The characteristic of a child is innocence, but remember there is a difference between the innocence of an ordinary child and the innocence of the babe of Bethlehem. Natural innocence is based on ignorance, and as life goes on things awaken and prove that innocence is not purity, it is not based on an unsullied foundation. Profoundly speaking, a child is not pure, and yet the innocence of a child charms us because it makes visible all that we understand by purity.

Growing Integrity

> And the LORD God commanded the man, saying, "Of every tree of the garden you may freely eat; but of the tree of the knowledge of good and evil you shall not eat; for in the day that you eat of it you shall surely die." (Genesis 2:16–17; see 2 Corinthians 11:3)

Integrity means the unimpaired state of anything. The golden ignorance manifested in our Lord's childhood and boyhood was unimpaired when He reached manhood and was manifested in a growing integrity. Jesus Christ carried out all that Adam failed to do, and He did it in the simple way of obedience to His Father. It is not the passing of the years that matures the life of the Son of God in us, but obedience. As we obey we find that all the power of God is at our disposal, and we too can grow in spiritual beauty. Are we humble and obedient, learning as Jesus learned, or are we hurrying into experiences we have no right to? If we have to find reasons for doing what we do, we should not do it. The life of a child is one of simple obedience. We grow spiritually by obeying God through the words of Jesus being made spirit and life to us and by paying attention to where we are, not to whether we are growing or not. We grow spiritually as our Lord grew physically, by a life of simple, unobtrusive obedience. If we do not obey God's Word and pay attention to the circumstances He has engineered for us, we shall not grow in spiritual beauty, but will become lopsided; our integrity will be impaired by something of the nature of inordinate lust. Remember, lust can be spiritual. Lust disputes the throne of God in us: "I have set my mind to this, or that, and I must have it at once." That will lead to gross experience. It means there is some desire, some inordinate affection or imagination we are not bringing into captivity to the obedience of Christ.

The soul in spiritual beauty must be a born-again soul, that is, something has come into it from without. The miracle described in Luke 1:35, "Therefore, also, that Holy One who is to be born will be called the Son of God," is the symbol of what happens when the Holy Spirit comes into us: the natural life is made the mother of the Son of God. We have to nourish the life of the Son of God in us, and we do it by bringing the natural life into accordance with His life and transforming it into a spiritual life by obedience.

Grand Invincibility

> And I will put enmity between you and the woman, and between your seed and her Seed; He shall bruise your head, and you shall bruise His heel. (Genesis 3:15; see Romans 16:19–20)

When we begin our lives with God, we wish He would make it impossible for us to go wrong. If He did, our obedience would cease to be of value. When God created man, He put into his hands the free choice of good or evil, and that choice is there still, and the very test develops the character. The basis of life is antagonism in every domain, physical, mental, moral, and spiritual; we only maintain health by fighting. Naturally we are not virtuous, but innocently ignorant. Disinclination to sin is not virtue any more than innocence is purity. The danger is to make a virtue of necessity. It is fighting that produces virtue, moral stability on the inside. Virtue has character at the back of it, it has been tested and tried and has triumphed. Spiritual stability within produces holiness. Our Lord was invincible as a Man: "Who is worthy to open the scroll and to loose its seals? . . . You are worthy to take the scroll and to open its seals" (Revelation

5:2, 9). Jesus Christ proved Himself worthy not only in the domain of God which we do not know, but in the domain of man which we do know. By means of His redemption Jesus Christ makes us the sons and daughters of God, and we have to put on the new man, in accordance with the life of the Son of God formed in us, and as we do we become invincible—"more than conquerors through Him who loved us" (Romans 8:37).

"I want you to be wise in what is good, and simple concerning evil" (Romans 16:19). The apostle Paul's counsel fits on exactly with Genesis 3:15. By obeying the life that was in Him, Jesus Christ manifested the wisdom of the serpent and the harmlessness of the dove. If we know good only by contrast with evil, we shall have the devilishness of the serpent through gross experience. But when we know good and evil in the way Jesus Christ knew them, all our subtle wisdom is on the side of the good and our dovelike nature is toward evil. When we are born again we have to obey the Spirit of God, and as we draw on the life of Jesus and learn to assimilate and carry out what He speaks to us, we shall grow in ignorance of certain things and be alive and alert only to what is God's will for us.

The Temple of God

Desecration

> Then Jesus went into the temple and began to drive out those who bought and sold in the temple, and overturned the tables of the money changers and the seats of those who sold doves. (Mark 11:15; cf. John 2:13–17)

We bring to the New Testament a sentimental conception of our Lord; we think of Him as the meek and mild and gentle Jesus and make it mean that He was of no practical account whatever. Our Lord was "gentle and lowly in heart" (Matthew 11:29), yet watch Him in the temple—meekness and gentleness were not the striking features there. We see instead a terrible

Being with a whip of small cords in His hands, overturning the money changers' tables and driving out men and cattle. Is He the meek and gentle Jesus there? He is absolutely terrifying; no one dared interfere with Him. Why could He not have driven them out in a gentler way? Because passionate zeal had "eaten Him up," (John 2:17) with a detestation of everything that dared to call His Father's honor into disrepute. "Do not make my Father's house a house of merchandise" (John 2:16)—the deification of commercial enterprise. Everything of the nature of wrong must go when Jesus Christ begins to cleanse His Father's house.

If you have been laid hold of by the Spirit of God, don't think it strange concerning the spring-cleaning God is giving you, and don't clamor for anything because it will have to go. The setting apart of my body by the Holy Spirit for a temple of God is a terror to everything in me that is not of God. Sensuality and sordidness lurk about the bodily temple until Jesus Christ cleanses it. Sensuality is that which gratifies my particular senses, it is the working of my body in connection with external circumstances whereby I begin to satisfy myself. Sensuality may be unutterably disgusting or it may be amazingly refined, but it is based on the wrong thing and has to go; it can have nothing to do with the temple of God, that is, with man as God created him.

My body is designed to be "the temple of the Holy Spirit" (1 Corinthians 6:19), and it is up to me to stand for the honor of Jesus Christ in my bodily practices. When the Spirit of God comes in, He cleanses the temple and does not let one darling sin lurk. The one thing Jesus Christ insists on in my bodily life is chastity. As individuals we must not desecrate the temple of God by tampering with anything we ought not to tamper with; if we do, the scourge of God will come. As soon as the Spirit of God comes in we begin to realize what it means—everything that is not of God has to be turned clean out. People are surprised and say, "I was told God would give the Holy Spirit to them that ask Him; well, I asked for the Holy Spirit and expected that He would bring me joy and peace, but I have had a terrible time ever since." That is the sign He has come, He is turning out the money changers and the cattle, that is, the things that were making the temple into a trafficking place for self-realization. We soon find why the gospel can never be welcome. As long as we speak winsomely about the meek and gentle Jesus, and the beautiful ideas the Holy Spirit produces when He comes in, people are captivated, but that is not the Gospel. The gospel does away with any other ground to stand on than that of the Atonement. Speak about the peace of heaven and the joy of the Lord and men will listen to you; but tell them that the Holy Spirit has to come in and turn out their claim to their right to themselves and instantly there is resentment—"I can do what I like with my body; I can go where I choose." The majority of people are not blackguards and criminals living in external sin; they are clean living and respectable, and it is to such that the scourge of God is the most terrible thing because it reveals that the natural virtues may be in idolatrous opposition to God.

> Jesus . . . overturned . . . the seats of those who sold doves. (Mark 11:15)

I may not be giving way to sensuality and sordidness, but I may be crooning a dirge of self-pity; doves in a cage are always cooing, "Oh, it is so hard for me, you don't know what I have to give up; doing the will of God is such an enormous cost." Consecration by the Spirit of God means merciless dealing with that kind of thing. He has no sympathy with it. How can we be of the slightest use to God if we are always whining about our own condition? The compromise arising from self-pity is quite sufficient to extinguish the whole purpose of God in a life

> And would not allow anyone to carry wares through the temple" (Mark 11:16)

The Spirit of God will not allow me to use my body for my own convenience; the whole limit must be God's. I am not to serve my own ends with my body; I am to serve the ends of Jesus Christ and be a devoted disciple of His. Lust (the spirit of I must have this thing at once) can have no part or lot in the house of God. So many spend their time in educating themselves for their own convenience, "I want to educate myself and realize myself." I must not use the temple of God for the convenience of self-love; my body must be preserved from trafficking for myself. One of the hardest scourges of God comes just here.

> Then He taught, saying to them, "Is it not written, 'My house shall be called a house of prayer for all nations'? But you have made it a "den of thieves.' " (Mark 11:17)

Have I been doing this? What has my soul been busy with during this past year? What have I been thinking in my mind and imagination? I may have been talking about holiness, but what has it meant to me? Is my body the temple of the Holy Spirit and am I taking care to see that it is? Is my imagination and reasoning and thinking regarded as the house of God? Or am I making it a house of merchandise—making it more for me and mine? wanting to go through this in order to grasp something for myself? God does not use us as an exhibition of what He can do. Jesus Christ said, "I am . . . the truth" (John 14:6); therefore the temple of my body must be consecrated to Him. The temple was to be the house of prayer for all the nations, and my personal life is to be the same. God will bring some extraordinary people to traffic through our temples. Think how we have trafficked through Him! Natural affinities do not count for anything in the spiritual life, but only the affinities produced by the Spirit of God (cf. 1 John 1:7).

Desolation

> O Jerusalem, Jerusalem, the one who kills the prophets and stones those who are sent to her! How often I wanted to gather your children together, as a hen gathers her chicks under her wings, but you were not willing! See! Your house is left to you desolate. (Matthew 23:37–38)

The historic temple was twice cleansed by our Lord; then when He came again to Jerusalem He no longer spoke of it as "My Father's house," but, "See! Your house is left to you desolate"—a terrible pronouncement—and a terrible possibility in our own lives. It is appallingly true that we may get to the place where Jesus can no longer say of us, "My Father's house," where He can no longer give us the benefit of scourging and cleansing but can only retire, a weeping Christ, over our willfulness. "How often I wanted . . . and you were not willing!" You have spurned and despised every messenger I sent, and now I say to you, "You shall see Me no more till you say, 'Blessed is He who comes in the name of the LORD' " (verse 39).

Is yours a desolated life, deserted in soul? Then in plain honesty don't blame your father or mother or anyone in your family; don't blame the fact that you had no education or that someone thwarted you when you were sixteen or that you were heartbroken when you were twenty-four or had a business disaster when you were thirty. These things may be facts, but they are not to the point. Nothing that transpires outside me can make the tiniest difference to me morally unless I choose to let it. The desolation described by Jesus was brought on by the people of God themselves and by them alone. Is God saying to you, "You have spurned and hated and murdered My messengers?" If so, it will be a painful thing for your desolated soul to say, "Blessed is He who comes in the name of the LORD"—Blessed is the one who stabs and hurts and disillusions me as to where I am.

A sinner who has never been cleansed by the direct act of the Lord may hear the gospel and receive the Holy Spirit who will do all the cleansing. Compare that condition with one who has backslidden, one who had been cleansed by God, but has allowed the traffic to get back, the sensuality, the self-seeking, the self-interest—the cattle are all back, the doves and the money-changers' tables—with a deepened and increased element of thieving. It is no longer making more for me and mine it is a downright thieving of God's time and opportunities and God's sacredness in other lives. That is what a spiritual thief does. Such a soul has to come back to God in desolation. It is no use to tell the backslider to receive the Holy Spirit—he cannot; the Holy Spirit will not be received by him; he has to come back to God in desolation. In the parable of the two sons, some of the elements in the parables of the lost sheep and the lost coin are missed out—the shepherd goes to seek the lost sheep and the woman searches for the lost coin but the father does not go to the far country; the son has to leave the pigs and what pigs eat and come back. And if you have backslidden you will have to do the same. "O Israel, return to the LORD your God, for you have stumbled because of your iniquity; take words with you, and return to the LORD. Say to Him, 'Take away all iniquity; receive us graciously' " (Hosea 14:1–2). Take words with you and say, "By my iniquity I have fallen, by lust, by worldliness, by self-interest"—you know exactly what it is. You have been trying to find comfort here and there and you will never get it; your soul is night, your heart is steel; you have spurned and trodden under and despised God's messengers, and you will only see God when you say, "Blessed is He who comes in the name of the LORD." Then, says God, "I will heal their backsliding, I will love them freely; for My anger has turned away from him" (Hosea 14:4).

Dedication

> Do you not know that you are the temple of God and that the Spirit of God dwells in you? If anyone defiles the temple of God, God will destroy him. For the temple of God is holy, which temple you are." (1 Corinthians 3:16–17)

Am I prepared to recognize that my body is a temple of the Holy Spirit? You say, "I did not know there were so many things in my life unsuited to the temple of God." Then let God turn them out—"I don't know whether He will." You do. Can you not tell when Jesus Christ lays His scourge on the back of the thing that should not be there? Never for one moment sympathize with anyone who says, "I don't know how to get to God." There is no one in the world more easy to get to than God. Only one thing prevents us from getting there, and that is the refusal to tell ourselves the truth. Am I prepared to receive the Holy Spirit? prepared to recognize that my body and soul and spirit are meant to be presented with divinity? Jesus Christ did not live and die to be our example only, but that He might put us in the place where He is by means of His wonderful atonement. Reverence your own body and soul and spirit for this one purpose, and reverence everyone else's for the same purpose.

Dedication means "setting apart to some sacred purpose." The historic temple was to be the house of prayer for all the nations, and my body and soul and spirit is to be God's house of prayer, preserved for devotion. I have to realize that my body is the temple of the Holy Spirit, the place where the work of intercession is carried on. Prayer based on the redemption creates what could not be until the prayer is offered. The Spirit needs the nature of a believer as a shrine in which to offer His intercessions. My personality, as far as I am conscious of it, and a great deal more than I am conscious of, is the shrine of the Holy Spirit. Have I recognized that it is? If I have, I shall be amazingly careful to keep it undefiled for Him. I am responsible before God for conducting my body as the temple of the Holy Spirit. Am I doing it, or is my body dictating to God, telling Him what it must do? If I only want God to keep my body healthy, He never will; I have to govern and rule my body as a temple of the Holy Spirit. "Therefore do not let sin reign in your mortal body, that you should obey it in its lusts" (Romans 6:12). When I become a Christian I have exactly the same body as before, but I have to see that my members, which were used as servants of sin, are now used as servants of righteousness. (see Romans 6:13). The apostle Paul tells us how it is done; he says, "I discipline my body and bring it into subjection" (1 Corinthians 9:27), until bodily senses and spiritual intuitions work together smoothly and naturally. Our bodies are not our shame, but our glory, and if we keep them as temples of the Holy Spirit we shall find that "the life of Jesus [will] be manifested in our mortal flesh" (2 Corinthians 4:11).

We have to recognize that the personal life is meant for Jesus Christ, that we have been designed not for ourselves, but for our Lord and Master. "If anyone desires to come after Me, let him deny himself, and take up his cross, and follow Me" (Matthew 16:24). How significant is our Lord's insistence on His own person in relation to human destiny. The modern jargon is all for self-realization; we educate ourselves for the purpose of self-realization, we select our friendships for self-realization purposes. Jesus says, "Whoever loses his life for My sake"—deliberately flings it away—"will find it" (Matthew 16:25). The one, great, dominant recognition is that my personal self belongs to Jesus Christ. The counterfeit is giving ourselves as devotees to a cause. Thousands of people are losing their lives for the sake of a cause; this is perilously wrong because it is so nearly right. Anything that rouses us to act on the line of principles instead of a relationship to a person fosters our natural independence and becomes a barrier to yielding to Jesus Christ. Have we recognized that our bodies are temples of the Holy Spirit, or are we jabbering busybodies so taken up with Christian work that we have no time for the Christ whose work it is; no time for Him in the morning, no time for Him at night, because we are so keen on doing the things that are called by His name? What we have to watch today is the competition of causes against devotion to Jesus Christ. One life, yielded to God at all costs, is worth thousands only touched by God. "Let him . . . take up his cross, and follow Me." What is the cross? The cross is the deliberate recognition of what my personal life is for, namely, to be given to Jesus Christ; I have to take up that cross daily and prove that I am no longer my own. Individual independence has gone, and all that is left is personal, passionate devotion to Jesus Christ through identification with His Cross. "Do you not know . . .you are not your own? For you were bought at a price; therefore glorify God in your body" (1 Corinthians 6:19–20).

Arriving at Myself

By the Surgery of Providence
(*his senses*)
But when he came to himself. (Luke 15:17)

It is difficult to realize that it is God who arranges circumstances for the whole mass of human beings; we come to find, however, that in the providence of God there is, as it were, a surgical knife for each one of us because God wants to get at the things that are wrong and bring us into a right relationship to Himself. At first we trust our ignorance and call it innocence; we trust our innocence and call it purity until God in His mercy surrounds us with providences that act as an alchemy transmuting things and showing us our real relation to ourselves. To say, "Oh, I'm sick of myself," is a sure sign that we are not. When we really are sick of ourselves we will never say so but will gladly come to the end of ourselves. So long as we say, "I'm tired of myself," it is a sign that we are profoundly interested in ourselves.

The Sin of Self-Importance

"Father, give me the portion of goods that falls to me." So he divided to them his livelihood. (Luke 15:12)

This is a picture of one who has become spiritually independent; the portion of goods from the Father has been received, there has been a real experience of God's grace, but there is the letter *I* about it, a self-assertive determination to carry things out in my own way. The most powerful type of spiritual delusion is produced in this way; it is based on ignorance of what we should do with the substance the Father has given us: we should devote it absolutely to Him. If we forget this we are certainly in danger of the sin of self-importance. It begins with the realization that God does do His recreating work through us if we are children of His—"Yes, God did use me," you say. God will use anything or anyone (cf. Matthew 7:21–23). Unless there is abandonment to the Lord Jesus, self-importance will always be inclined to utilize God's blessing for its own ends. No man can abandon to Jesus Christ without an amazing humiliation to his own self-importance. We are all tremendously important until the Holy Spirit takes us in hand; then we cease to be important and God becomes all-important.

The Sordidness of Self-Indulgence

> And not many days after, the younger son gathered all together, journeyed to a far country, and there he wasted his possessions with prodigal living. (Luke 15:13)

The soul that has claimed its portion and become spiritually independent may ultimately be degraded into feeding pigs and eating with them. More awful things are said about backsliding than about any other sin. If we do not maintain a walk in accordance with the perception given, we shall fall as degradingly low as we were high before. The depth of degradation is measured by the height of attainment. Don't deal with it on the surface and say, "I'm not built that way, I have none of those sordid tastes." The nature of any dominating lust is that it keeps us from arriving at a knowledge of ourselves. For instance, a covetous man will believe he is very generous. Thank God for the surgery of providence by means of which He deals with these absurdities. The way God brings us to know ourselves is by the kind of people He brings round us. What we see to condemn in others is either the discernment of the Holy Spirit or the reflection of what we are capable of ourselves. We always notice how obtuse other people are before we notice how obtuse we ourselves are. If we see meanness in others, it is because we ourselves are mean (see Romans 2:1). If we are inclined to be contemptuous over the fraud in others it is because we are frauds ourselves. We have to see ourselves as God sees us, and when we do it keeps us in the right place: "My God, was I ever like that to You? so opinionated and conceited, so set on my own ends, so blind to myself?" These things, which are most unpalatable, are true nevertheless. Beware of any belief that makes you self-indulgent; it comes from the pit, however beautiful it sounds. It is an indication of a wrong relationship that does not spring from the attitude of abandon, and we become perverse and remain ignorant of the fact that we need to be guarded by God.

The Sorrow of Self-Introspection

> But when he came to himself, he said, "How many of my father's hired servants have bread enough and to spare, and I perish with hunger!" (Luke 15:17)

There is no pain on earth to equal the pain of wounded self-love. Unrequited love is bad enough, but wounded self-love is the cruelest thing in human life because it shifts the whole foundation of the life. The prodigal son had his self-love wounded; he was full of shame and indignation because he had sunk to such a level. There was remorse but no repentance yet, no thought of his father. "I will arise and go to my father, and will say to him, 'Father I have sinned against heaven and before you, and I am no longer worthy to be called your son. . . .' And he arose and came to his father" (verses 18–20). That is repentance. The surgery of providence had done its work; he was no longer deluded about himself. A repentant soul is never allowed to remain long without being gripped by the love of God.

> Man, what is this, and why art thou despairing?
> God shall forgive thee all but thy despair.

Let the surgery of providence drive you straight to God. The Spirit of God works from the standpoint of God, from a standpoint inconceivable to the natural man. The words *miraculous* and *supernatural* are disliked today through the influence of modern psychology on spiritual work, that is, the attempt to define on psychical lines—materialistically psychical lines—how God works in a soul. The surgery of the providence of God will break up all ignorance of ourselves. It is impossible for a human being to guard his unconscious personality; only God can do it. If we have not abandoned to Jesus Christ we are likely to be trapped on every hand by our complete ignorance of ourselves and panic will result. Panic leads us away from the control of God and leaves us not only beyond our own control, but possibly under the control of other forces. The one safeguard is abandonment to the Lord Jesus, receiving His Spirit, and obeying Him.

By the Surprises of Personality

> And the glory which You gave Me I have given them, that
> they may be one just as We are one. (John 17:22)

My Right to My Individual Self

> If anyone desires to come after Me, let him deny himself,
> and take up his cross, and follow Me. (Matthew 16:24)

The natural is not sinful, neither is it spiritual; the ruling disposition of my personality makes it either sinful or spiritual. The natural life and individuality are practically one and the same. Individuality is the characteristic of a child, it is the natural husk of personality, and it is there by God's creation to preserve the personal life; but if individuality does not become transfigured by the grace of God, it becomes objectionable, egotistical, and conceited, interested only in its own independence. When natural independence merges into independence of God it becomes sin, and sin isolates and destroys and ultimately damns the personal life. Jesus Christ lays His axe at the root of independence. There is nothing dearer to the heart of the natural man than independence. Wherever there is authority, I go against it in order to show I am independent; I insist on my right to myself, my right to an independent opinion. That spirit does not fit in with Jesus Christ at all. Independence and pride are esteemed by the natural man, but Jesus says, "what is highly esteemed among men is an abomination in the sight of God" (Luke 16:15).

The statements of Jesus about discipleship produce embarrassment in the natural man: "From that time many of His disciples went back and walked with Him no more" (John 6:66). If we are to be disciples of Jesus Christ, our independent right to our individual selves must go—and go altogether. We evade the claims of Jesus by saying they have a mystical meaning and we try to get away from their intensely practical rugged meaning. "If anyone desires to come after Me," said Jesus, "let him deny himself," that is, deny his right to his individual self. Our Lord always mentions the most intimate relationships in connection with discipleship, relationships that make human life what it is by the creation of God, and He implies that any one of these relationships may enter into competition in some form or other with His call; if they do, He says it must be prompt obedience to Him. It is not only sin that awakens resentment in the natural heart of man to the claims of Jesus Christ, but individuality that has been abused by the disposition of sin. The Holy Spirit continually urges us to sign away our right to the individual self to Jesus. "Learn from Me," says Jesus, "for I am gentle and lowly in heart" (Matthew 11:29). How few of us do learn from Him! We cling to our individuality like a drowning man to a straw—"Of course God will recognize my individual peculiarisms and prejudices." Jesus Christ pays attention to one thing only: "If you would be My disciple, deny your right to yourself." Individual peculiarisms are excrescences belonging to the husk of the personality and are the things that produce all the difficulty. When the disposition of sin has been dealt with by identification with the death of Jesus, the natural individual life still remains.

Individuality must be transfigured by the indwelling of the Holy Spirit and that means a sword going through the natural. Over and over again the Holy Spirit brings us to the place that in evangelical language is called "full surrender." Remember what full surrender is. It is not giving up this thing and that, but the deliberate giving up of my right to my individual self. As long as we are slaves to our ideas of individuality we distort the presentation of our Lord's teaching about discipleship.

The Recognition of My Personal Self

> He who finds his life will lose it, and he who loses his life for My sake will find it. (Matthew 10:39)

We have to recognize that the personal life is meant for Jesus Christ. The modern jargon is for self-realization—"I must save my life"—Jesus Christ says, whoever "loses his life for My sake will find it." The cross is the deliberate recognition of what our personal self is for, namely, to be given to Jesus, and we take up that cross daily and prove we are no longer our own. Whenever the call is given for abandon to Jesus Christ, people say it is offensive and out of taste. The counterfeit of abandon is that misleading phrase, *Christian service*. I will spend myself for God, I will do anything and everything but the one thing He asks me to do—give up my right to myself to Him. But surely Christian service is a right thing? As soon as we begin to say that, we are off the track. It is the right person, the Lord Jesus Christ, not the right thing—don't stop short of the Lord Himself: "for My sake." The great, dominating recognition is that my personal self belongs to Jesus. When I receive the Holy Spirit, I receive not a possible oneness with Jesus Christ, but a real, intense oneness with Him. The point is, will I surrender my individual life entirely to Him? It will mean giving up not only bad things, but things that are right and good (cf. Matthew 5:29–30). If you have to calculate what you are willing to give up for Jesus Christ, never say that you love Him. Jesus Christ asks us to give up the best we have got to Him—our right to ourselves. There is only this one crisis and in the majority of lives it has never been reached; we are brought up to it again and again and, every time, we go back. Self-realization must be renounced in order that Jesus Christ may realize Himself in us.

The Realization of Christian Self

> I indeed baptize you with water unto repentance, but He who is coming after me is mightier than I, whose sandals I am not worthy to carry. He will baptize you with the Holy Spirit and fire. (Matthew 3:11)

This is neither the individual self nor the personal self, but the Christian self. "That they may be one just as We are one" (John 17:22). How is this oneness to come about? by the baptism of the Holy Spirit and in no other way. When the Spirit of Jesus comes into me He comes into my personal spirit and makes me incandescent with God. The individual peculiarisms are seen no longer but only the manifestation of oneness with God. One person can merge with another person without losing his identity, but an individual remains definitely segregated from every other individual. When the disciples were baptized by the Holy Spirit they became witnesses to Jesus (see Acts 1:8; 4:13). When a man falls in love his personality emerges and he enters into relationship with another personality. Love is not anything for me at all; *love* is the deliberate giving of myself right out to another, the sovereign preference *by* my person for another person. The idea, I must have this person for myself, is not love, but lust. Lust counterfeits love in the same way that individuality counterfeits personality. The realization of the Christian self means that Jesus Christ is manifested in my natural life—not Christian sentiment, but Christian self. Individuality is not lost, it is transfigured by identification with the person of Jesus.

Is there any use in beating about the bush? We call ourselves Christians; what does our Christianity amount to practically? Has it made any difference to my natural, individual life? It cannot unless I deliberately give up my right to myself to Jesus and as His disciple begin to work out the personal salvation He has worked in. Independence must be blasted right out of a saint. God's providence seems to pay no attention whatever to our individual ideas because He is after only one thing—"that they may be one just as We are one." It may look like a thorough breaking up of the life, but it will end in a manifestation of the Christian self in oneness with God. Sanctification is the work of Christ in me, the sign that I am no longer independent, but completely dependent upon Him. Sin in its essential working is independence of God; personal dependence upon God is the attitude of the Holy Spirit in my soul.

The Saints in the Disaster of Worldliness

> Here is the patience of the saints; here are those who keep
> the commandments of God and the faith of Jesus.
> (Revelation 14:12)

The language of the book of Revelation is easily
misunderstood. For instance, when we use the word *beast* we
mean something particularly offensive to our sensibilities; the
"beast" in the book of Revelation is anything but offensive; he is
not an immoral beast, socially understood, but a beast from God's
standpoint.

The Patience of the Enshrined Life of God

Here is the patience of the saints. The revelation of God in the
Bible works in a twofold way: first the incarnate fact, our Lord
Jesus Christ; second, the interpretation of that fact enshrined in
the lives of those who are called to be saints. A saint is one in
whom the life of Jesus Christ is formed.

The description given in Revelation 14:9–11 is the
description of prosperous worldliness such as has never been
seen before, but from God's standpoint it is a moral disaster, and I
should say we are very near the type of civilized life that this
refers to. What is described in the climax is true in every stage
until the climax is reached. After the war, this combine of
everything, in which it will be impossible to have religion

independent of an organization or business independent of a federation, will take place.

In the Perversion of Religion

> If anyone worships the beast and his image, and receives his mark on his forehead or on his hand . . . . (Revelation 14:9)

This is the description of a man who has given the best he has got to the ruling power that gives him what he wants. If he is consecrated entirely there, he will meet with undoubted prosperity. He receives a mark on his forehead, or upon his hand (symbols of thought and grasp), a mark of the time in which he lives, cut off from everything other than the present order of things. The worship that should be given to God is given to the beast and his image. The saint has to endure, keeping "My command to persevere" (Revelation 3:10), maintaining the enshrined life of God in the midst of this perversion of religion. We can always recognize the mark of the Beast if we apply this one simple test—was it necessary for Jesus Christ to have lived and died to produce that attitude to life?

In the Punishment of Revelation

> . . . he himself shall also drink of the wine of the wrath of God, which is poured out full strength into the cup of his indignation. (Revelation 14:10)

Intoxicated by the elemental wrath of God! The love of God and the wrath of God are obverse sides of the same thing. If we are morally rightly related to God we see His love side, but if we reverse the order and get out of touch with God, we come to a place where we find everything is based on wrath—not that God is angry, like a Moloch, but wrath is inevitable; we cannot get out of it. If we give the best we have got to worldliness we shall one day wake up to the revelation of what we have done and shall experience the wrath of God, mingled with ungovernable despair: "I gave the best I had got, not to God, but to the world, and I can't alter now." This is not only true with individuals, but with the whole of civilized life. Take the good, thoroughgoing, prosperous, worldly business people of any country who have worshiped at the shrine of a pagan worldliness, you will find exactly what Jesus says, their hearts fail them—"men's hearts failing them from fear and the expectation of those things which are coming on the earth" (Luke 21:26). Men who have worshiped mammon have the mark of the Beast in thought and grasp and, when the realization of where they are comes, they faint for fear. Civilizations will get there, and the panic in any country will be beyond all limits. God is the controller of history.

In the Pain of Recession

> And the smoke of their torment ascends forever and ever.
> (Revelation 14:11)

That is the pictorial way of presenting the atmosphere of the wrath in which civilizations will be found when God is manifested. When medieval artists wanted to portray a crime they usually accompanied the scene with bad weather. According to God's Book, this is not merely pictorial, but a representation of what will actually take place. "The smoke of their torment" refers not only to the physical condition of individuals, but to the terrific disturbance in nature that is connected with it. Satan is the prince of the power of the air.

Take the popular idea of Christianity and compare it with the patience of the saints, and you will see where we are. Popular Christianity says, "We must succeed." The book of Revelation says success cannot be marked, it is impossible. The New Testament conception of spirituality in the world is a forlorn hope always, by God's design. Take the parable of the sower (which is the key to all the parables), only one-fourth of the seed sown brings forth fruit in this dispensation. We are determined to be successful; the apostle Paul says we are called upon to be faithful (1 Corinthians 4:1-2). In this dispensation it is a day of humiliation in the lives of the saints as it was in the life of our Lord. We have to remain steadfastly patient to God through the whole thing.

The Practice of the Expressed Love of God

Here are those who keep the commandments of God. What are the commandments? "The first of all the commandments is: '. . . you shall love the LORD your God with all your heart, with all your soul, with all your mind, and with all your strength'. . . . the second . . . is this: 'You shall love your neighbor as yourself' " (Mark 12:29-31).

Among the Unseemly

Love . . . does not behave rudely [unseemly KJV]. (1 Corinthians 13:4-5). In prosperous worldliness there is any amount that is unseemly, not from the social standpoint, but from the saint's standpoint. The way worldly sagacity argues is, "pay men back in their own coin; if you have been deceived, deceive in order to get your rights"—in other words, "an eye for an eye and a tooth for a tooth" (Matthew 5:38). You cannot do that if you are a saint. We must practice the expressed love of God and behave among the rude as the children of God. There is no test on earth to equal it. There is rude laughter at the saint—"Where is your success? What have you done? What is the good of missionary enterprise? What is the use of talking about spiritual things to soldiers?" If the saints are not practicing the expression of the love of God, they will be discouraged and give up. Discouragement is disenchanted egotism: "I have not got what I wanted, therefore I am not going on, I give it up. I have lost my conceit."

Love . . . thinks no evil (verse 5). It does not ignore the fact that there is evil, but it does not take it into calculation. Someone has done us a wrong, and we say, "Now I must be careful." Our attitude is to be that of the expressed love of God, and if we take the evil into account we cannot express His love. We must deal with that one as God has dealt with us. There is no bigger, stiffer job for a saint than that.

Among the Unspiritual

Love . . . does not rejoice in iniquity, but rejoices in the truth (verse 6). Prosperous worldliness is unspiritual and those who do not pray and who are not at all holy get on well. There is so much nervous energy spent in spiritual exercises, in giving time to study, that the temptation is to let these things slip. We have to express the love of God and see that we do not become unspiritual among the unspiritual tendencies around us. If you listen to the talk of the day in which we live, you find it is sagacious common sense that rules, the spiritual standpoint is taboo, like a fairy story. The question is whether we will maintain the spiritual standpoint or say, "Oh, yes, it is rather too high"? We do not need Jesus Christ and the Bible for the ordinary commonsense standpoint, and if in a crisis we act according to common sense we do not express the love of God.

Among the Unshameable

Love . . . bears all things . . . endures all things (verse 7). After every phase of a particular type of successful civilized life, we get the anticonventionalist who tries to develop the unshameable attitude and brags about things. It is called pluck. It is not; it is shamelessness, and it is easy to remain unspiritual before that.

At the basis of every one of these matters, the unseemly, the unspiritual, the unshameable, is something that is right, a strong basis of common sense; the test for the saint is not common sense, but, "Is this what Jesus Christ stood for?" "For I am not ashamed of the gospel" (Romans 1:16), says the apostle Paul. If you dare to stand for Jesus Christ and His presentation of things in certain crises, men will separate you from their company, treat you with unutterable contempt. "Blessed are you," said Jesus, "when men hate you, and when they exclude you, and revile you, and cast out your name as evil, for the Son of Man's sake" (Luke 6:22). We have to express the love of God in the midst of these things.

The Power of the Enshrouded Loyalty to God

and the faith of Jesus (Revelation 14:12). The faith of Jesus is exhibited in His temptation and can be summed up in His own words: "I do not seek My own will but the will of the Father who sent Me" (John 5:30). Jesus remained steadfastly loyal to His Father, and the saint has to keep the faith of Jesus.

Under the Success of Civilization (Matthew 4:3–4)

In the temptation the sagacity of Satan is seen from every standpoint—"If You are the Son of God, command that these stones become bread" (Matthew 4:3), that is, "Look after men's bodies, feed them and heal them, and you will get men under Your control." Was Satan right? would Jesus Christ have gained the Kingship of men if He had put their needs first? Read John 6:15: "Therefore when Jesus perceived that they were about to come and take Him by force to make Him king, He departed again to the mountain by Himself alone." It is this temptation that has betaken the Christian church today. We worship man, and God is looked upon as a blessing machine for humanity. We find it in the most spiritual movements of all. For instance, watch how subtly the missionary call has changed. It is not now the watchword of the Moravian call, which saw behind every suffering heathen the face of Christ; the need has come to be the call. It is not that Jesus Christ said "Go," but that the heathen will not be saved if we do not go. It is a subtle change that is sagacious but not spiritual. The need is never the call. The need is the opportunity. Jesus Christ's first obedience was to the will of His Father:

"Behold . . . in the scroll of the book it is written of Me. I delight to do Your will" (Psalm 40:7–8). and, "As the Father has sent Me, I also send you" (John 20:21). The saint has to remain loyal to God in the midst of the machinery of successful civilization, in the midst of worldly prosperity, and in the face of crushing defeat.

Under the Success of Ceremonialism (Matthew 4:5–7)

"If You are the Son of God, throw Yourself down." In other words, "Do some supernatural wonder, use apparatus whereby You will paralyze men's wits and stagger them, and the world will be at Your feet." In the midst of the success of worldliness we get an outburst of spiritualism, of supernaturalism, fire called down from heaven by the authority of the devil, and all kinds of signs and wonders whereby people say, "Behold, here is Christ." Jesus said, "The kingdom of God does not come with observation" (Luke 17:20). I believe in the Second Coming but not always in its advocates. They are apt to ignore altogether what Jesus said.

Under the Success of Compromise (Matthew 4:8–10)

"All these things will I give You if You will fall down and worship me." As if to say, "Be diplomatic, be wise, compromise in a wise, shrewd way and You will get everything under Your own control." That is the kind of thing the peace of the world is based on—we call it "diplomacy." Jesus maintained His faith in God's methods in spite of the temptations that were so sagacious and wise from every standpoint, except the standpoint of the Spirit of God. The insinuation of putting men's needs first, success first, has entered into the very domain of evangelism and has substituted the passion for souls for the passion for Christ, and we experience shame when we realize how completely we have muddled the whole thing by not maintaining steadfast loyalty to Jesus Christ.

You will find the things God uses not to develop you, but to develop the manifestation of God in you are just the things we are apt to ignore—successful worldliness, other people, trials of our faith—these are the things that either make a saint unsaintly or give God the chance to exhibit Himself. The most delightful saint is the one who has been chastened through great sorrows. The type of character produced by great sorrows is different from that produced by the pressure of the "mosquito" order of things. The saints are unnoticed; there is no flourish of trumpets about them, nothing self-advertized, but slowly and surely this characteristic comes out—the stamp of a family likeness to Jesus Christ, and men realize that they have been with Jesus (see Acts 4:13).

"Out of the Wreck I Rise"

Yet in all these things we are more than conquerors through Him who loved us. (Romans 8:37)

God does not do what false Christianity makes out—keep a man immune from trouble; there is no promise of that. God says, "I will be with him in trouble." The moral frontier where Jesus Christ works is the great, dominant note in the New Testament; the external manifestation comes later. At present it is the relationship on the inside that is being dealt with—the personal preference of the soul for God, which is the great fruit of Christianity. No matter what actual troubles in the most extreme form get hold of a man's life, not one of them can touch the central citadel, namely, his relationship to God in Christ Jesus.

This is one of the greatest assets of the spiritual aspect of Christianity, and it seems to be coming to the fore just now. Before the War it may have been imaginary to talk about these things in the universal sense but now they are up-to-date in thousands of lives. The "wrecks" are a fact. Moral, physical, and spiritual wrecks are all around us today. The apostle Paul is not talking of imaginary sentimental things, but of desperately actual things, and he says we are "more than conquerors" in the midst of them all, superconquerors, not by our wits or ingenuity, our courage or pluck, or anything other than the fact that not one of them can separate a man from the love of God in Christ Jesus, even though he should go into the belly of hell. We are inclined to ask God to do the magic business, to perform a miracle that will alter our external circumstances, but if we are ever going to understand what the God whom Jesus Christ presents is like, we have to remember that that is not His first job. The first thing God does is to alter a man's disposition on the inside and then enable him to deal with the mess on the outside. God never coerces a man—he has to take God's way by his own moral choice; we reverse the order and demand of God that He do our work. The tawdry things that have been presented as the findings of Christianity make one impatient.

The Cares of Tribulation

> Who shall separate us from the love of Christ? (Romans 8:35)

Shall tribulation? The word *tribulation* has its root in the Latin *tribulum*—a sledge for rubbing out corn, literally, a thing with teeth that tears. Christianity is not prayer meetings and times of fellowship; these are magnificent and essential in certain conditions for the manifestation of the Christian life, but when tribulation is tearing you to bits, they cannot be. Tribulation describes a section of a man's life. Rightly or wrongly, we are exactly in the condition we are in. I am sorry for the Christian who has not some part of his circumstances he wishes was not there! People with psychological "elbows" bring tribulation. Let the tribulations be what they may—exhausting, galling, fatiguing—they are never noble things, Beelzebub miseries that buzz over the windows of a man's soul so that he cannot see out—we can be "more than conquerors" in them if we maintain our belief in the relationship God has to us in Christ Jesus.

"To him who overcomes . . ." (Revelation 2:7, 17; 3:21): God does not give us the overcoming life; He gives life to the man who overcomes. If, in every case of tribulation from gnats to the cruelty of the sword, we take the step as if there were no God to assist us, we shall find He is there. The idea is not that we get the victory, but that the Victor has got us. "Now thanks be to God who always leads us in triumph in Christ, and through us diffuses the fragrance of His knowledge in every place" (2 Corinthians 2:14).

The Waters of Anguish

or anguish? Anguish comes from a word meaning to press tightly, to strangle, and the idea is not a bit too strong for the things people are going through. They are not sentimental things, but real things, where every bit of a man's life is twisted and wrung out to the last ebb. Can the love of God in Christ hold there, when everything says that God is cruel to allow it and that there is no such thing as justice and goodness? Shall anguish separate us from the love of God? No, we are more than conquerors in it, not by our own effort, but by the fact that the love of God in Christ holds. If we look for God in the physical domain we shall see Him nowhere; if we look for Him in the kingdom on the inside, in the moral relationships, we shall find Him all the time. We lose faith in God when we are hurt in the physical domain and God does not do what we want; we forget that He is teaching us to rely on His love. Watch some people and you will wonder how a human being can support such anguish; instead of being full of misery, they are the opposite. They seem to be held by a power that baffles all human intelligence, to have a spiritual energy we know nothing of—what accounts for it? "When you pass through the waters, I will be with you . . . . When you walk through the fire, you shall not be burned" (Isaiah 43:2). The waters are real, and the fire is real, but in Romans 8 Paul claims that the relationship to God holds.

"And you will hear of wars and rumors of wars. See that you are not troubled" (Matthew 24:6). When men's hearts are fainting for fear, does Jesus Christ expect us to be undisturbed? how is it to be done? have we to become callous and indifferent or so worn out that we have not enough vitality to feel things? Jesus Christ means that the relationship He can bring us into with Him can hold us undisturbed in the midst of every disturbance there is—if there is anything supernatural, that is! Human pluck cannot stand these things, there is a limit. No human being can stand calamity and anguish without going under or getting into a panic. Panic is a sudden terror, our whole beings get into a flutter and we don't know where to turn; we can take a forlorn stand, but it barely stills the panic inside. If we are going to be more than conquerors in calamity, it can only be in the marvelous way by which God ships in the supernatural and makes it natural.

The Mutinies of Persecution

or persecution? As soon as we get hold of a particular thing in the spiritual domain we are going to be systematically vexed by those who don't intend us to have it; they are set on gibing it out of us because if we are right, they are wrong. Mutiny, a rise against authority, comes from persecution. There is any amount of weakness in us all, but deep down there is red-handed rebellion against the authority of Jesus Christ—"I'll be damned before I yield." Don't take a poetical view of things that go beyond science. At bottom, sin is red-handed mutiny that requires to be dealt with by the surgery of God—and He dealt with it on Calvary.

The Specter of Famine

or famine? Can a man remain true to the love of God when he is famine-stricken? God does not prevent physical suffering because it is of less moment than what He is after. "And do not fear those who kill the body but cannot kill the soul" (Matthew 10:28). Famine is a most appalling specter; it means extreme scarcity. Can I not only believe in the love of God, but be more than conqueror while I am being starved? Either the apostle Paul is deluded and Jesus Christ is a deceiver, or some extraordinary thing happens to a man who can hold on to the love of God when the odds are all against His character.

The Scare of Poverty

or nakedness? The scare of poverty is the most effectual onslaught. If we know that obedience to God means absolute poverty, how many of us would go through with it? The scare of poverty will knock the spiritual backbone out of us unless we have the relationship to God that holds. It is easy to fling away what you have, child's play to sell all you have got and have nothing left, the easiest piece of impulse, nothing heroic in it; the thing that is difficult is to remain detached from what you have so that when it goes you do not notice it. That is only possible by the power of the love of God in Christ Jesus.

The Cruelty of the Sword

or peril, or sword? In every one of "these things" logic is shut up. A logic-monger can silence the man who is suffering with his facts, but suppose the man who is suffering has got hold of reality and the logic-monger finds he is only slinging actualities? Did you ever try to justify God in what He allows? God is not justified unless He can work things out on the line Paul brings out, and we only get there by a moral revolution. The one who deals with the logical, rational side has the best of the argument just now though not the best of the facts, and one of the biggest humiliations is that you cannot say a word; you must let the chattermagging go on. You can shut the mouth of the man who has faith in God, but you cannot get away from the fact that he is being kept by God. That is a domain that logic must shut out resolutely until it is realized that logic is an instrument only. A man can go through tribulations that make you hold your breath as you watch him; he goes through things that would knock the wits out of us and make us give way to blasphemy and whimperings. He is not blind or insensitive, yet he goes through in marvelous triumph—what accounts for it? one thing only: the fact that behind it all is the love of God which is in Christ Jesus our Lord. Spiritually, morally, and physically the saint is brought clean through, triumphant, out of the wreck wrought by tribulation, anguish, persecution, famine, nakedness, peril, and sword. Whatever may be the experiences of life, whether terrible and devastating or monotonous, it makes no difference; they are all rendered impotent because they cannot separate us from the love of God, which is in Christ Jesus Our Lord. "Out of the wreck I rise" every time.

The Conditions of Spiritual Life

Matthew 10:24–42

Religion is a matter of taste, a matter in which a man's religious life and his actual life do not necessarily agree. In spiritual life that could never be; spiritual life means the real life, and it is significant that whenever Jesus talks about discipleship He speaks of it in actual terms.

"It is enough for a disciple that he be like his teacher" (Matthew 10:25). At first sight this looks like an enormous honor—to be like his teacher is marvelous glory—is it? Look at Jesus as He was when He was here—it was anything but glory. He was easily ignorable except to those who knew Him intimately; to the majority of men He was as a root out of dry ground (see Isaiah 53:2). For thirty years He was obscure, then for three years He went through popularity, scandal, and hatred; He succeeded in gathering a handful of fishermen as disciples, one of whom betrayed Him, one of whom denied Him, and all of whom forsook Him; and He says, "It is enough for you to be like that." The idea of evangelical success, church prosperity, and civilized manifestation does not come into it at all. When we fulfill the conditions of spiritual life we become unobtrusively real.

The Dear Sorrows of Spiritual Difference
verses 24–26

A disciple is not above his teacher. (verse 24)

When we become spiritual there is a change in us that our former companions feel but cannot locate; they intuitively sense that something is different, there is something that does not agree with their natural outlook. It is a most embarrassing difference in the closest relationships of life (see Matthew 10:22–23). Our affinity with Jesus Christ does make a difference; it produces sorrow and misunderstandings, things that cannot be explained. But Jesus says when misunderstandings arise, "Don't be afraid, one day it will be understood how it came about." Meantime we have to lay our account with the sorrows of spiritual difference, but our devotion to Jesus is so intense that no matter what those sorrows are, we are prepared to go through with it.

The Defiant Sagacity of Spiritual Discretion
verses 27–28

Whatever I tell you in the dark, speak in the light. (verse 27)

There are dark nights in the soul; darkness is the time to listen. If we are to be true to the conditions of spiritual life we must speak not what is expedient, we must speak the truth regarding spiritual realities. The Christianity that is not spiritual says we must by no means offend or do anything that hurts a Christian brother's feelings. Did Jesus ever offend anyone knowingly? He certainly did (see Matthew 12:1–8); but He never put a stumbling block in anyone's way. The sagacity of spiritual discretion does not mean we have to be obstinate and pigheaded, with a curse of finality about our views, or that we preach what is expedient—"Oh, yes, I agree with you, but it is not expedient to say that kind of thing in public." If God has given us the revelation it is not our business to hide our light under a bushel (Matthew 5:15–16). In your sagacity be wise. Don't preach out of natural discretion, but out of spiritual discretion that comes from intimacy with God. The prophet is more powerful than the priest or king, and in our Lord the prophet element is the great one.

Jesus never spoke with the sagacity of a human being, but with the discretion of God. Beware of saying what is expedient from your own commonsense standpoint, especially when it comes to the big truths of God.

The Detailed Security of Spiritual Dependence
verses 28–31

> Do not fear those who kill the body but cannot kill the soul. (verse 28)

"Do not fear those who kill the body"—leave that alone, but beware of being disobedient to your own spiritual stand before God because that will kill both body and soul, that is, make you reprobate. Watch, if in the tiniest degree you begin to be afraid. "Now what is going to happen to me physically, in matters of money, in my social circumstances, if I do obey Jesus?" Jesus distinctly says, "Pay no attention to that, beware only of being destroyed both physically and spiritually by disobedience." Whenever we get out of touch with spiritual reality our bodies instantly suffer. The source of physical strength in spiritual life is different from what it is in natural life. In natural life we draw our strength direct from without; in spiritual life we draw our physical strength, consciously or unconsciously, from communion with God. When that is broken, physical health begins to be destroyed. Jesus says, "Your Father, who looks after the sparrows, will care for you; therefore, do not fear (see verse 29). It is not to be a life of self-interest at all. When God calls us He never gives security; He gives us a knowledge of Himself. We reveal how much we believe in the things Jesus said when we reason like this: "Is this God's will for me? No, it can't be because there is no security." "It is enough for a disciple that he be like his teacher." Jesus never had any home of His own, never a pillow on which to lay His head. His poverty was a deliberate choice. We may have to face destitution in order to maintain our spiritual connection with Jesus, and we can only do that if we love Him supremely. Every now and again there is the "last bridge"—"I have gone far enough, I can't go any further." If you are going on with God, it is impossible to secure your interests at all. We have to go on in perfect confidence that our Father in heaven knows all about us. Are we prepared to fulfill these conditions when they arise?

The Dreaded Stand of Spiritual Destiny
verses 32–33

> Therefore whoever confesses Me before men . . . . (verse 32)

When I am born from above not only is the Holy Spirit in me, but the Son of God is formed in me (Galatians 4:19), and to *confess* Him means that I allow His disposition to have its way through my bodily life; ". . . him I will also confess before My Father who is in heaven." Will He? or will He have to say, "There is not one detail of your life that has manifested Me. I have had no chance of looking through your eyes, of working through your hands, or loving through your heart." The true evangelist is the one whose life in every detail overflows with the manifested life of Jesus (cf. Matthew 7:22–23). The world has a right to say, "Produce your goods." In actual circumstances we can prevent Jesus Christ being hurt if we take the blow, but if we stand on our rights the blow goes back on Him. It is not aggressive doing on our part that wins, but the manifestation that it is the Lamb who breaks the seals. (see Revelation 5–6). If we stand for Jesus Christ we have to take care to nourish His life in us, to bear His name; then, He says that He will confess us before His Father who is in heaven.

The Suffering of Spiritual Discipleship
verses 34–39

> I did not come to bring peace but a sword. (verse 34)

It never costs a disciple anything to follow Jesus; to talk about cost when you are in love with someone is an insult. The point of suffering is that it costs other people—fathers, mothers, households; consequently we decline to go on, consideration for others causes us to hold back. If we go on with it, then others will suffer. Have we, in effect, told Jesus we are not prepared for this? "Obedience to Your call would mean I should get into difficulties with my home, my father, my mother, and I cannot possibly be the means of bringing suffering on them." Jesus says, "If you are going to be My disciples, you must be prepared to." God knows what it costs them and what it costs you to allow it.

The Solidarity of Spiritual Discipline
verses 40–42

> He who receives you receives Me. (verse 40)

Solidarity means a consolidation or a oneness of interests. Here, the solidarity is between us and God; we deliberately identify ourselves with God's interests in other people. "Inasmuch as you did it to one of the least of these My brethren, you did it to Me" (Matthew 25:40).

The Sacrament of Saints

I

I am the living bread which came down from heaven. If anyone eats of this bread, he will live forever; and the bread that I shall give is My flesh . . . for the life of the world. (John 6:51)

Why should I start at the plow of my Lord, that maketh deep furrows on my soul? I know He is no idle husband-man, He purposeth a crop.

Samuel Rutherford

Good corn is not bread; if we are compelled to eat corn we will suffer for it. Corn must be ground and mixed and kneaded and baked, and baked sufficiently, before it is fit to be eaten. When the husk is away and the kernel garnered, we are apt to think that all is done, but the process has only just begun. A granary of corn is not bread; people cannot eat handfuls of corn and be nourished, something must be done to the corn first. Apply that illustration to the life of a sanctified saint. The afflictions after sanctification are not meant to purify us, but to make us broken bread in the hands of our Lord to nourish others. Many Christian workers are like Ephraim, "a cake not turned" (Hosea 7:8); they are faddists and cranks, and when they are given out for distribution they produce indigestion instead of giving nourishment.

The Way of the Plow (Matthew 13:18-23)

> Therefore hear the parable of the sower. (Matthew 13:18)

It is the plow that prepares the ground for sowing the seed. The hard way through the field is the same soil as the good ground, but it is of no use for growing corn because it has never been plowed. Apply that to your own soul and to the souls of men. There are lives that are absolutely stupid toward God, they are simply a way for the traffic of their own concerns. We are responsible for the kind of ground we are. No man on earth has any right to be a high road; every man has the chance of allowing the plow to run through his life. Sorrow or bereavement or conviction of sin, anything that upsets the even, hard way of the life and produces concern, will act as the plow. A man's concern about his eternal welfare witnesses that the plow has begun to go through his self-complacency. The words of our Lord, "Do not think that I came to bring peace on earth. I did not come to bring peace but a sword" (Matthew 10:34), are a description of what happens when the gospel is preached—upset, conviction, concern, and confusion.

The Wildness of the Place (Genesis 3:17-19)

> Then to Adam He said, ". . . cursed is the ground for your sake; in toil you shall eat of it all the days of your life." (Genesis 3:17)

That is a description of the place where the plow has to go. It was once a holy place, but now it is desecrated and wild. "The heart is deceitful above all things, and desperately wicked; who can know it?" (Jeremiah 17:9). The way through the field that has been battered hard by men's feet is an illustration of the human heart. The human heart should be the abode of God's Holy Spirit, but it has been trampled hard by passions until God has no part in it, and the plow has to come into the desecrated place. As workers we must remember this fundamental line. The tendency today is to ignore it, to say that men do not need plowing, they need praising; that the human heart is not bad; that the world is not a wild place. The plow has to come into every place that has been desecrated by the prince of this world, for one purpose—for the seed to be sown.

The Work of Patience (Galatians 6:7)

> Do not be deceived, God is not mocked; for whatever a man
> sows, that he will also reap. (Galatians 6:7)

Don't sow the human heart with mingled seed: "You shall not sow your field with mixed seed" (Leviticus 19:19). God's seed will always bring forth fruit if it is put in the right conditions. Man cannot order the seasons or make the seed to grow (cf. Jeremiah 33:20), and as preachers and teachers we are powerless to make saints. Our duty is to put the seed into the right place and leave the rest to God. It would be foolish for a farmer to sow his seed and tell his servants to watch it; he must sow his seed in the right place and then trust in God and nature, and by and by he will reap his harvest. So all we can do is to sow the seed of the Word of God in the hearts of the hearers. The words our Lord uttered in reference to Himself are true of every seed that is sown—"Unless a grain of wheat falls into the ground and dies, it remains alone; but if it dies, it produces much grain" (John 12:24). All Christian work, if it is spiritual, must follow that law because it is the only way God's fruit can be brought forth.

Be endlessly patient. There is nothing more impertinent than our crass infidelity in God. If He does not make us plowers and sowers and reapers all at once, we lose faith in Him. Modern evangelism makes the mistake of thinking that a worker must plow his field, sow the seed, and reap the harvest in a half hour. Our Lord was never in a hurry with the disciples, He kept on sowing the seed and paid no attention to whether they understood Him or not. He spoke the truth of God and by His own life produced the right atmosphere for it to grow and then left it alone because He knew well that the seed had in it all the germinating power of God and would bring forth fruit after its kind when it was put in the right soil. We are never the same after listening to the truth; we may forget it, but we will meet it again. Sow the Word of God, and everyone who listens will get to God. If you sow vows, resolutions, aspirations, emotions, you will reap nothing but exhaustion. "And you shall sow your seed in vain, for your enemies shall eat it" (Leviticus 26:16); but sow the Word of God, and as sure as God is God, it will bring forth fruit. Human sympathy and human emotions and human hypnotism in preaching are the signs of a spiritual hireling and a thief. Sow emotions, and the human heart will not get beyond you. There are men and women at work for God who steal hearts from God—not intentionally, but because they do not preach the Word of God. They say, I don't want anyone to think about me; that should never need to be said. If the thought of ourselves is lurking anywhere as we preach, we are traitors to Jesus Christ. Our duty is to get people through to God. A man may not grasp all that is said, but something in him is intuitively held by it. If you talk truth that is vital to you, you will never talk over anyone's head. See that you sow the real seed of the Word of God, and then leave it alone.

II

A grain offering . . . shall be . . . an offering made by fire, a sweet aroma to the LORD. (Leviticus 2:2)

This Scripture in Leviticus 2, as in fact all Scripture, testifies that service is self-surrender, self-sacrifice. Christ, to satisfy others, was broken; the bread-corn must still be bruised; and the nearer our ministry approaches the measure of His ministry—immeasurably far as we shall ever be behind Him—the more shall we resemble Him, the bruised, the oppressed, the broken One.

Reaping

Corn that has come to fruition must be watched. The enemy of souls works most havoc in the standing corn. Our Lord told the disciples to "pray the Lord of the harvest to send out laborers into His harvest" (Luke 10:2), to cut down the corn, that is, to disciple men and women. God puts in His sickle by the hand of a disciple and cuts us down where we never thought we would have to be cut down. Every sanctified soul is handed over by God to a disciple to be reaped for Him. What do we say to the people who have come into the experience of sanctification—"Thank God, you are all right now?" That is not discipling them. People come in to reap who have no right to reap. We have to let sanctified souls know that they are there to be cut down, to be reaped, to be made into bread to feed the world. We are apt to shout *Hallelujah!* when souls enter into sanctification, but it is then that a time of intense care and anxiety begins until these lives are reaped for God. The need is to watch the standing corn, to watch those who are right with God until they are matured and established. Notice the earnest solicitation Paul had for his converts: "My little children, for whom I labor in birth again until Christ is formed in you" (Galatians 4:19). The time after sanctification in every soul under our care is an additional concern to us if we are true servants of God. Times of revival have led the church to rejoicing instead of watching by earnest prayer until these souls are reaped. Never sympathize with cut down souls, but rejoice, and teach them to rejoice.

"For what is our hope, or joy, or crown of rejoicing? . . . For you are our glory and joy" (1 Thessalonians 2:19–20). This is the dividing of the spoil. How many of us are going to hear Jesus Christ say when we stand before Him, "That soul was reaped by you?" Jean MacLean wrote underneath the only photograph she ever had taken, "Spoilt for this world saving as I can win souls to Jesus." She was an obscure, noble missionary and was used by God in untold numbers of lives, she literally reaped them for God.

Threshing

The first description John the Baptist gives of Jesus is that of a Divine Husbandman at work in His threshing floor (see Matthew 3:12). When corn is stored in the granary we are apt to think that that is the end, but it is only the beginning. Sanctification is a reaping, an end, but also a beginning. Standing corn has to be cut down and to go through the processes of reaping, threshing, grinding, mixing, and baking before it is good for food; sanctified souls must be told that their only use is to be reaped for God and made into bread for others. It is time we got away from all our shallow thinking about sanctification. The majority who are introduced into an experience of sanctification remain at the gateway—saved and sanctified—but they do not know how to go on; consequently they begin to stagnate. We need to learn that God has a lot to do with a saint after sanctification; our perplexities come because this is not realized. We have to see that as right dividers of the Word of truth, we bring this before people.

Beware of being guided by mental or spiritual affinities, let God mix you as He sees fit. Peter thought he knew better than God, but God had to mix Peter with the Gentiles before he became good bread (see Acts 10:9–16).

Grinding

Jesus said that in the lives of the saints there will be tribulation; not difficulties, but tribulation. The great cry of modern enterprise is success; Jesus says we cannot be successful in this age. This is the age of the humiliation of the saints; that means we have to stand true to Jesus Christ while the odds are crushingly against Him all the time.

"Tribulation produces perseverance" (Romans 5:3). In the experience of tribulation we are brought to understand what millstones are. Millstones are used to grind the corn to powder, and they typify the sacredness of the discipline of life: "No man shall take the lower or the upper millstone in pledge, for he takes one's living in pledge" (Deuteronomy 24:6). You have been having a snug time in the granary, then God brings you out and puts you under the millstones, and the first thing that happens is the grinding separation our Lord spoke of—"Blessed are you when men . . . cast out your name as evil, for the Son of Man's sake" (Luke 6:22). The other crowd want to have nothing more to do with you, you are crushed forever out of any resemblance to them. Very few of us know anything about suffering "For My sake." When God is putting His saints through the experience of the millstones, we are apt to want to interfere. Hands off! No saint dare interfere in the discipline of the suffering of another saint. God brings these things into our lives for the production of the bread that is to feed the world.

In the East the women sing as they grind the corn between the millstones, and the sound of the millstones is music in the ears of God. The worldling does not think it music, but the saint who is being made into bread knows that his Father knows best and that He would never allow the suffering if He had not some purpose. Ill-tempered people, hard circumstances, poverty, willful misunderstandings, and estrangements are all millstones. Had Jesus any of these things in His own life? He had a devil in His company for three years; He lived at home with brothers and sisters who did not believe in Him; He was continually thwarted and misunderstood by the Pharisees—and He says, "a disciple is not above his teacher" (Matthew 10:24). If we have the tiniest element of self-pity in us God dares not put us anywhere near the millstones. When these experiences come, remember God has His eyes on every detail.

Baking

There is a spiritual significance in the methods of preparing the meal offering mentioned in the book of Leviticus (chapter 2)—in the frying pan, seething in pots, or baking in an oven. Why some people suffer is open and clear to everyone; others are placed in a boiling tumult (watch a porridge pot and you will see what this means), and only God knows what is happening. Others are placed in fierce, silent ovens; no one knows what is going on, but when they are taken out they are precious to God and to man alike. God is producing good food for Himself and for His saints. We all have our special functions—never try to do what someone else is doing; let God make you what He wants you to be. He knows your circumstances and He will alter them when He chooses. As a saint be careful of God's honor.

III

He who sows the good seed is the Son of Man. The field is the world, and the good seeds are the sons of the kingdom. (Matthew 13:37–38)

Be content, ye are His wheat growing in our Lord's field. And if wheat, ye must go under our Lord's threshing instrument, in His barn-floor, and through His sieve, and through His mill to be bruised, as the Prince of your salvation, Jesus, was (Isaiah 53:10), that ye may be found good bread in your Lord's house.

Samuel Rutherford

God sows His saints in the most useless places—according to the judgment of the world. Where they will glorify Him is where God puts His saints, and we are no judge at all of where that is. When we become rightly related to God the likelihood of our being of use to men seems in the eyes of the world to be pathetically crippled. People say, "Don't be so absurd as to go and bury yourself there." We have to let God sacrifice us as He likes, and go where He sends us. Never be deluded into making this statement: "I am here because I am so useful"; say rather, "I am here because God wants me here." The one lodestar of the saint is God Himself, not estimated usefulness.

Blessed Bread: Sacrificed

> And He took the five loaves and the two fish, and looking
> up to heaven, He blessed and broke and gave the loaves to
> the disciples; and the disciples to the multitudes." (Matthew
> 14:19; cf. Romans 12:1)

God never uses in His service those who are sentimentally devoted to Him; He uses only those who are holy within in heart and holy without in practice. The book of Leviticus is full of spiritual teaching, and the significance of all the detail is that a servant of God must keep himself unspotted from the world, sternly and guardedly holy, not for his own sake, but for the sake of his calling. No man has any right to break the Word of God and feed the people of God unless he is without blemish spiritually through the Atonement. That standard is being blotted out nowadays. "And no man takes this honor to himself" (Hebrews 5:4)— nearly all do, though. Preaching is worthy in God's sight when it costs something, when we are really living out what we preach. The truth of God is to be presented in such a way that it produces saints.

Broken Bread: Suffering

> And as they were eating, Jesus took bread, blessed and
> broke it, and gave it to the disciples and said, "Take, eat; this
> is My body." (Matthew 26:26; cf. 1 Peter 4:19)

Not only does God waste His saints, according to the judgments of men, He seems to bruise them most mercilessly. You say, "But it could never be God's will to bruise me." If it pleased the Lord to bruise His own Son, why should He not bruise you? To choose suffering is a disease, but to choose God's will even though it means suffering is to suffer, as Jesus did, according to the will of God.

In the Bible it is never the idealizing of the sufferer that is brought out, but the glorifying of God. God always serves Himself out of the saint's personal experience of suffering. If suffering is used to idealize the sufferer there is an aftermath of sickly sentimentality—"What I have gone through!" and God is not glorified. In actual life the true sufferers and the affected sufferers are mixed, and the Spirit of God gets His chance only through the one or two who are so completely effaced by means of identification with the death of Christ that the thought of what they are going through never affects them. The thing that strikes one about such lives is never the sense of restraint but of inspiration, the feeling that there is unfathomably more behind.

If we are self-willed when God tries to break us and will do anything rather than submit, we shall never be of any use to nourish other souls; we shall only be centers of craving self-pity, discrediting the character of God. Jesus called self pity satanic (see Matthew 16:22–23). No one understands a saint but the saint who is nearest the Savior, and if we accept sympathy from any others, we will end in being traitors to Jesus Christ because the reflex thought is, "Well, God is dealing hardly with me." The people we have to knit to our souls are not those who sympathize with us—they hinder because sympathy if it is from a wrong source always enervates—but those who bring us into a fuller realization of the purpose of God.

Jesus Christ represents the bread of God broken to feed the world, and the saints are to be broken bread in His hands to satisfy Jesus Christ and His saints. When by the sanctifying power of the grace of God we have been made into bread, our lives are to be offered first of all to Jesus Christ. "Give Me a drink" (John 4:7). In the Old Testament the firstfruits were always offered to God, and that is the symbol for our lives. The saint is meant to satisfy the heart of Jesus first, and then be used to feed His saints. "And you shall be witnesses to Me" (Acts 1:8)—a perfect delight to Me wherever I place you. The saints who satisfy the heart of Jesus make other saints strong and mature for God. The one characteristic of the life is: "In all the world there is none but thee, my God, there is none but thee."

The consummation of self-sacrifice is that just as our Lord was made broken bread and poured-out wine for us, so He can make us broken bread and poured-out wine for others; but He cannot do it if there is anything in us that would make us give way to self-pity when He begins to break us. The one mainspring of the life is to be personal, passionate devotion to Jesus Christ.

Beatified Bread: Sovereignty

> For I consider that the sufferings of this present time are not worthy to be compared with the glory which shall be revealed in us. (Romans 8:18; cf. Ephesians 2:6)

The saints who satisfy the heart of Jesus are the imperial people of God forever; nothing deflects them, they are super-conquerors, and in the future they will be side-by-side with Jesus. "To him who overcomes, I will grant to sit with Me on My throne, as I also overcame and sat down with My Father on His throne" (Revelation 3:21). The glorified Lord will take up His abode with the saint who puts God first in reality, not in sentiment. "We will come to him and make Our home with him" (John 14:23)—the triune God abiding with the saint! Jesus Christ is made heavenly bread to us now, and there is a glorious day coming—and is even now the experience of many of His people—when the nourishment of the life is the same for the saint as for his Lord. "I will come in to him and dine with him, and he with Me" (Revelation 3:20).

Note to the Reader

The publisher invites you to share your response to the message of this book by writing Discovery House Publishers, Box 3566, Grand Rapids, MI 49501, USA. For information about other Discovery House books, music, or videos, contact us at the same address or call 1-800-653-8333. Find us on the Internet at http://www.dhp.org/ or send e-mail to books@dhp.org.

The Oswald Chambers Library

Spiritual guidance from the author of *My Utmost for His Highest.*
Powerful insights on topics of interest to every believer:

My Utmost for His Highest
Updated Edition—hardcover
Prayer Edition (Original)—hardcover
Large Print Edition (Original)—softcover

My Daily Journey With My Utmost for His Highest
by Carolyn Reeves
A companion to the golden book of Oswald Chambers

Baffled to Fight Better
Job and the problem of suffering

Biblical Psychology
Christ-centered solutions for daily problems

Bringing Sons Into Glory &
Making All Things New
The glories of the great truths of salvation and redemption

Christian Disciplines
Build strong Christian character through divine guidance,
suffering, peril, prayer, loneliness, and patience.

Daily Thoughts for Disciples
A collection of 365 daily readings from the best of a variety
of Chambers' writings

The Highest Good &
The Shadow of an Agony
Seeing life from God's perspective

If You Will Ask
Reflections on the power of prayer

The Love of God
    An intimate look at the Father-heart of God

Not Knowing Where
    A spiritual journey through the book of Genesis

The Place of Help
    God's provision for our daily needs

Prayer: A Holy Occupation
    A comprehensive collection of Chambers' writings on
prayer

Studies in the Sermon on the Mount
    God's character and the believers conduct

Shade of His Hand
    Ecclesiastes and the purpose of life

So Send I You &
Workmen of God
    Recognizing and answering God's call to service

About Oswald Chambers

Oswald Chambers: Abandoned to God by David McCasland
    The life story of the author of *My Utmost for His Highest,* this
volume unveils Chambers' active, devout, Christ-centered life
from which flowed this century's best-loved devotional book.

Order from your favorite bookstore or from:

Discovery House Publishers
Box 3566
Grand Rapids, MI 49501

Call toll-free: 1-800-653-8333